THE CIVIL WAR ON CONSUMER RIGHTS

THE CIVIL WAR ON CONSUMER RIGHTS

Laurence E. Drivon

with Bob Schmidt

Conari Press
Berkeley, California

Excerpts from *Liability: The Legal Revolution and its Consequences* by Peter W. Huber (New York: Basic Books Inc., copyright © 1988 by Peter Huber) are reprinted with permission.

ISBN: 0-943233-06-2

Library of Congress Catalog Card Number: 89-81241

The book is dedicated to my brothers and sisters of the trial bar. Give up? They never have, they never will.

CONTENTS

ACKNOWLEDGMENTS

Special thanks to my wife, Georgia, for her tolerance and to Will Glennon who provided invaluable assistance.

PREFACE

"The first thing we do, let's kill all the lawyers."

William Shakespeare put those words into the mouth of one of his characters some 400 years ago. Dick the Butcher, in The Second Part of King Henry the Sixth, appears to have had very little, if anything, to do directly with lawyers in his turbulent life. It was <u>rules</u> he didn't like, and in his mind, it was lawyers who wrote the rules and meted out the punishment if they weren't obeyed. Do away with lawyers, and you do away with rules, and that was okay with Dick and his fellow revolutionaries.

There are modern counterparts of Dick the Butcher, but they are considerably more sophisticated, subtle, and clever. They don't like lawyers and they don't like rules—at least, they don't like the rules they themselves haven't made up—but instead of saying "Do away with lawyers," they suggest doing away with what lawyers do, or rather, with what *some* lawyers do. The lawyers who attract this disaffection are the plaintiff's attorneys, or trial lawyers; those who provide representation for consumers and working people who have become victims, who have suffered physical or emotional or economic injury because of the negligence or wrongdoing of another. The representation would be meaningless if it did not have an opportunity to be effective; fortunately for everyone in the United States who has ever been made a victim, a system exists that provides that anyone, rich or poor, can have effective representation.

Our civil justice system is one of the glories of our civilization. It provides a means to determine if wrongdoing or negligence has occurred, who is responsible if it has occurred, who should pay if compensation is appropriate, and how much. It shares one objective with the criminal justice system: It tries to make wrongdoing unprofitable. The civil justice system is the product of centuries of evolution, but its primary purpose today is the same as it has always been: the civilized settlement of disputes. There has always been another way to settle disputes, of course, a way considerably older than the civil justice system: the use of might, strength, power. Call it what you will, it has nothing at all to do with justice, with right.

This is a book about the law and our civil justice system. It contends the system is under attack, and the wagers of the war against the system are those elements in our society who have might, strength, power, and wealth, and who are displeased because in a courtroom their power and wealth give them no advantage at all over the least of us who claims to have suffered from another's negligence or wrongdoing.

Defenders of the civil justice system contend consumers are entitled to quality and value for their dollar, and sometimes the only way people get that is to sue the individual or institution that sold them goods or services that were not worth what was paid for them. Sometimes accidents occur because those goods or services are deficient in quality, and consumers suffer physical, emotional, or economic injury. Sometimes the individual or business responsible for injuries caused by defective goods or services refuses to acknowledge responsibility, and the only way to obtain compensation is for consumers to sue, to take the party they claim is responsible into court so accountability and the amount of compensation, if any, can be determined.

Opponents of the civil justice system have another view: Caveat emptor—let the buyer beware. Let the employee beware. In this view of the world, businesses that provide goods and services for the public and employers that determine the safeness of working conditions for their employees should not be held responsible if something goes wrong, if value and quality are not equal to the amount paid, if someone gets hurt or something is damaged because of negligence or a deficiency in quality.

Critics of our civil justice system declare that imposing accountability on manufacturers, hospitals and doctors, insurance companies, and other institutions and individuals stifles enterprise. The top official of a firm says a safe substitute for asbestos has been found, but the firm won't market the substitute in case it doesn't work and someone gets cancer and sues. Obstetricians say they're going to have to stop delivering babies unless they can be insulated from being sued if they make a mistake and cause a baby to die or suffer brain damage.

This book is about the battle raging between supporters of those two points of view. Supporters of the latter view, calling for little or no accountability, have been on the offensive for many years now and have scored some significant—and, I believe, frightening and detrimental—victories. My opinion, not surprisingly, is that if they continue to win, the rest of us lose. Not just trial lawyers, the most visible target of the offensive, but all of us.

This is a book about lawyers, the civil justice system, and the system's rules; and about the threats to them. It is intended to alert readers that the system being threatened is *their* system, that the rules that have been developed and are now in jeopardy are for *their* protection. The access to the civil justice system that is endangered is *their* access.

There are lawyers who are good and noble, and I will be

discussing mostly what those kinds of lawyers have accomplished. There are also, unfortunately, lawyers who are neither good nor noble, and I will also discuss their practices and suggest ways to recognize them.

Specific cases will be detailed to show how our existing legal system protects victims. No attempt is being made to collect a series of anecdotes simply for the purpose of showing that some manufacturers, some insurance companies, some doctors, either by design or through negligence, cause people pain. I acknowledge, sadly, that a book could be written compiling anecdotes showing that some lawyers, either by design or through negligence, cause people pain. I will try to show what, exactly, is really at risk from the so-called "tort reform" campaign being waged across the country by those interests who so often find themselves defendants in personal injury lawsuits.

Russ Herman, the 1989-90 president of the Association of Trial Lawyers of America, borrowing language from another Shakespeare character, calls the civil justice system's attackers "Beasts of Prey." Their lawyer-bashing, he says, is merely a means to an end. And the desired end, he said in a 1987 speech, is "a future without juries, plaintiff's lawyers, or conscience; a future which will guarantee that the Beasts of Prey undertake no risk in performing or underwriting negligence."

The campaign to create that frightening future seeks success by creating a public climate that will tolerate radical changes in the civil justice system. If the public can be persuaded that most lawyers are crooks, that most victims are malingerers, that most judges are senseless, that too many juries award too much money for trivial injuries, it could consent to "reforms" in the system. The "reforms" would change the rules that now create an equality in the courtroom; that, for example, force a giant corporation or a doctor or an insurance company or even a government to open its records to an ordinary person's lawyer.

This book is a personal statement for me because I am a trial lawyer who has practiced his profession with integrity and conviction for more than 20 years. I have never grown accustomed to the lawyer-bashing campaign my colleagues and I have had to endure, but I accepted it as part of the business. I don't expect the people and businesses I sue on behalf of a client to like being brought into court, and I understand when their unhappiness increases in direct proportion to the amount of the judgment against them.

But I've become aware that the constant trial lawyer-bashing has had a damaging impact on the public's respect for the law and the civil justice system, and that concerns me. If the public hears over and over and over again, and comes to believe, that trial lawyers lie, cheat, and steal, that they put their own interest ahead of their clients', that they use the law and its processes only as devices to satisfy their greed, that they bend and twist and convolute the law to achieve victory at the expense of truth and fairness, that they can't be trusted, the negative public attitude created will not be confined to trial lawyers. If the law and the civil justice system can be used in such wicked ways by such wicked people, then why should good and honest people believe they have value for them?

The wagers of the war think they will win if they succeed in diminishing respect for the law, and succeed in gaining support for their efforts to dismantle the civil justice system or to deny access by victims to that system. But if society is unable to provide justice to its members, nobody wins.

1

CIVIL JUSTICE IN
JEOPARDY

There is a war being waged in the United States today, a war without bullets and bombs, but a war nevertheless. And one of the sides doesn't even know a war is going on. It will learn about it—too late—if the other side wins.

The wealthiest, most powerful elements of our society—insurance companies, manufacturers, doctors and hospitals, and sometimes even governments—are the "other side." The war they are waging, a civil war, is against consumers and workers. What consumers and workers will lose, if they lose, is the equality the law now gives them with those wealthy, powerful elements.

At stake in this modern civil war is the legal recognition of one of the most fundamental of our values: accountability. As a people, we believe each of us is responsible for his or her actions, and for the consequences of those actions. We believe a child who breaks a window with a baseball should pay to replace it. We believe

19

a man and a woman each have a responsibility for any child they bring into the world. We believe a company that sells a product should stand behind the product and guarantee that it works as advertised. We believe a company that manufactures and sells a product so poorly designed or made that it injures or kills someone should be required to compensate the injured consumer or family and take the defective product off the market so that others won't be injured or killed. We believe a physician who commits malpractice should compensate the patient and, as much as possible, undo the harm done.

We believe these things and our forefathers believed these things, but for too much of our history the strong were able to fend off efforts to hold them accountable for injuries caused by their negligence or lack of concern for the safety of others. Despite the strength of our convictions, the legal pathways to justice were often obstructed by detours and dead ends. In the past the direction of the law, more often than not, was controlled and influenced by powerful interest groups. While they were more than willing to use the law when it was in their interest to do so, they demanded a system that at the same time protected them from unwanted legal assaults. In theory, there was equality under the law. In fact, the code books and court decisions were infested with "technicalities" that made it exceedingly difficult for an aggrieved individual who had suffered injury because of a shoddy product or an employer's disdain for worker safety to find justice in the courtroom.

During the second half of this century, in a series of legal developments stretching over several decades, the entrenched special interest bias of the law began to crumble. The crumbling is not complete, but enough has occurred so that accountability is now a fact of law. The weak are on an even legal footing with the strong. Ordinary people have the right—and the means—to demand that individuals and businesses and governments be held accountable for any injuries they have caused. Juries now have authority to determine if an injury has been suffered; if the accused individual, business, or government was responsible for the injury; and, if so, how much compensation, if any, should be given to the victim.

These changes were only rarely given to us through enlightened legislatures in our federal or state capitols. For the most part, the changes came about because determined individuals and a handful of equally determined trial lawyers took on the strong in the courtroom, and won. With these changes, and with the increased accessibility and skill of trial lawyers who were willing to represent wronged consumers on the condition that they would be paid only if they won, the modern era of consumer rights was born.

But the empowerment of individual consumers resulting from legal recognition of the concept of accountability has triggered a backlash from the powerful economic interests accustomed to relying on the protection of the law to avoid responsibility for consequences of their wrongdoing. The defense lobby—those who seem to find themselves frequently cast as defendants in personal or economic injury lawsuits—launched a campaign to overthrow that legal recognition of accountability.

The backlash was not simply an angry, mindless response to the equalizing of legal privilege. The campaign to turn back the legal clock began quietly in corporate board rooms and was artfully constructed to employ all the sophisticated marketing techniques perfected over the past 50 years of selling products and politicians. We are now in the midst of that carefully planned, long-term, nationwide, incredibly expensive campaign. The revolutionaries, the ones who initiated and launched the campaign, have chosen for their battleground the centuries-old body of law that maintains the balance of power between Corporate America and the public at large: the civil justice system. They want to take away the protection accountability gives to consumers and workers when they most

21

need it, when they are sick or injured or in desperate financial straits because of the actions of another.

And the attackers have selected for their weapon what they call "tort reform," a useful little phrase aimed at altering the civil justice system that holds them accountable and provides protections for consumers and working people. (A "tort" is a civil wrong, as distinguished from a criminal wrong.)

The phrase "tort reform" was not chosen by whim. Extensive public opinion sampling guided high-priced "spin doctors" (public relations and political consulting-type folks whose job it is to "spin" an issue to its most favorable side for their clients) to use this term that implies inefficiency and corruption, and predisposes a reader or listener to the need for change.

The wagers of the war can't come right out and disclose their intentions, of course; if they did, consumers and employees would be alerted to the danger that precious protections could be lost to them. To hide its real purpose, the lobby appeals to people's fears and prejudices.

Throughout the '80s and now into the '90s, the public was and is being subjected to a ceaseless series of "alarms" about a "litigation explosion," about avaricious lawyers who take advantage of soft-headed judges and fuzzy-thinking juries to extract huge, unrealistic awards from blameless defendants for the benefit of themselves and their mendacious clients. The alarms are found in books, magazine articles, and opinion pieces, and are heard in speeches across the land. The Congress and every state legislature are continually subjected to intense pressure to enact what the lobby's campaign managers call "tort reform."

The campaign's efforts take different forms and approach objectives in different ways, but all work toward the lobby's primary objective of eliminating altogether any risk to its members by denying to victims the right to bring them into court, or by denying to juries authority to hear evidence and make a determination of responsibility. "Tort reform" would accomplish this by making it more difficult for victims to find experienced trial lawyers to represent them. No lawyer, no lawsuit, no risk from having victimized someone.

There are three things individuals and corporations can do to avoid being sued, losing in court, and, possibly, hit with large punitive damage penalties. First, they can choose not to do the kinds of things that harm people and outrage juries. Or, if they have done them in the past and been sued and lost, they can choose not to do them in the future. Second, if they didn't want to worry about such liability, they could have a ceiling placed on the amount of damages a jury could award. The medical industry succeeded in doing that in California in 1975 with the Medical Injury Compensation Reform Act (MICRA). Third, they could also avoid liability by having such a low ceiling placed on the percentage of any award a lawyer could collect through a contingency fee agreement that experienced, competent lawyers would be discouraged from taking complex, time-consuming cases. All three of the insurance industry-sponsored initiatives on the November 1988 California ballot contained provisions capping the fees of plaintiffs' attorneys (but not, interestingly, the fees or salaries paid to defense lawyers).

I believe the great majority of individuals and firms that do business with the public have enough pride and economic common sense to avoid the risk that comes with turning out shoddy products, reneging on contracts, or providing careless service. Unfortunately, there are too many who choose, instead, to try alternatives two or three rather than deal fairly with the consumers of their products or services. Rather than deal fairly with the public, rather than perform on their contracts, rather than improve the quality of their products or services, rather than right the wrongs addressed by juries when they make awards, some individuals and businesses instead try to prevent juries from hearing the facts in a dispute in the first place; or, failing that, they try to restrict a jury's right to compensate a victim fully or impose appropriate punishment. And to use alternatives two and three, members of the lobby need "tort reform."

The campaign to diminish or eliminate accountability and risk via "tort reform" has enjoyed mixed success. Every state has enacted some of the elements in the basic tort reform package, but every defense lobby victory has prompted a furious retaliation by consumers when they realize what precious rights and protections have been stripped away from them.

Just to give you an idea of the scope of the battle, some of the "reforms" the defense lobby has succeeded in lobbying into law have subsequently been declared unconstitutional by courts in Washington, Florida, Arizona, Illinois, Idaho, Kansas, Louisiana, Minnesota, Montana, New Hampshire, North Dakota, Ohio, Oklahoma, Texas, Virginia, Michigan, Missouri, New Mexico, Pennsylvania, Rhode Island, Wyoming, Colorado, Georgia, Wisconsin, Kentucky, Alabama, North Carolina, South Dakota, Utah, Alaska, Hawaii, Nevada, South Carolina, Connecticut, and Iowa.

Courts in these and other states have also upheld the constitutionality of some provisions diminishing accountability, but the battle goes on. In 1986, the Connecticut Legislature enacted a far-reaching "tort reform" package described by the Conference of Insurance Legislators as a "model act." Connecticut is the home of the insurance industry in the United States, so it should not be surprising that the industry wields enormous influence over the Legislature in that state. Despite its clout, however, the industry was unable to prevent much of the "model act" being repealed a year later by legislators indignant because the promised benefits—lower insurance rates and increased availability—didn't materialize.

Despite the fact that what are in peril are rights and protections so much a part of our lives that their loss is almost beyond comprehension, not many people appreciate the significance of the battle being waged, or are even aware that a fight is taking place. That's not difficult to understand. For most people, the civil justice system is a blur of unintelligible code sections, court opinions, courtrooms, and lawyers. Even the term "tort law" is meaningless to most people. Tort law attempts to provide a just remedy for those victims of another's wrongdoing.

But tort law is the province of the civil justice system, a system our instincts tell us we should avoid. After all, to have reason to sue somebody (to become a plaintiff) a person must suffer a serious physical, emotional, or economic injury of some sort, and who wants to suffer serious injury? And certainly no one wants to be sued (and become a defendant).

Most of us have a natural aversion to the idea of placing our fate in the hands of impersonal laws, imposing judges, expensive lawyers, and solemn courtrooms. Certainly a part of that unease is a sense that the system is stacked against the little guy, that "you can't fight city hall." There is some basis for that; historically, it has indeed been difficult to beat city hall, much less any of our country's large and powerful economic interests.

Despite this natural aversion, however, we've come to rely on the civil justice system. We have succeeded in persuading people to turn to it for help, instead of taking the law into their own hands, when a wrongdoer refuses to acknowledge responsibility. It's still difficult for people to believe city hall can be beaten, but there is a growing awareness that it can be done. City hall and the country's large and powerful economic interests don't like that.

Many of the rules and rights and protections that we now take for granted were won for us by lawyers who took on what came to be landmark cases on a contingency fee basis for clients who had little or no money to spend on lawsuits. As we delve into some of these landmark cases later in the book, you'll find they have one thing in common: A business firm or government agency, wealthy and powerful outside the courtroom, was held accountable for injury done to an individual who was comparatively poor and weak outside the courtroom. They were held accountable because, inside the courtroom, the plaintiff and the defendant were of equal strength—they were balanced.

Our civil justice system works because it is balanced, because the parties using it voluntarily or involuntarily are equal to each other once inside the system. But the balance is delicate, so delicate that it can't stand abuse from any quarter. It can't stand abuse from greedy insurance companies making excessive profits, in part by refusing to pay benefits for which policyholders have contracted. It can't stand abuse from victims who file and pursue fraudulent claims or who exaggerate or lie about their damages. It can't stand legislative abuse by elected officials who abdicate their responsibility to deal with their constituents' problems and instead tangle themselves in political game playing. It can't stand abuse from greedy attorneys who misapply the system and surcharge it for their own gain.

There are abuses, unfortunately, so the system's balance is in constant peril. Add to that peril the danger from the attacks being launched by the defense lobby. The attacks are all the more dangerous because they are not direct, frontal assaults on the system itself, certainly not directly on our constitutionally guaranteed right to a trial by jury in civil matters. They are subtle, but they are constant.

Diminish trust in and respect for lawyers, and you accomplish the same end as a successful assault on the U.S. Constitution's Seventh Amendment. Change the rules to remove the incentive for lawyers to take complex, difficult cases and you accomplish the same end. Change the rules so that juries, outraged by a defendant's conduct, are limited in the punishment they can impose for that conduct, and you accomplish the same end.

More protection for the strong. Less protection for the weak. That is not the direction in which this country should be traveling.

2

WOMEN, THE
PROPERTY OF MEN?

A 21-foot-long, 630-pound pipe slipped from its defective support one September day in 1970 and fell on 22-year-old Richard Rodriguez, changing his life forever and setting in motion legal activity that eventually affected the life of every woman then living and yet to be born in California.

Richard Rodriguez's accident need not have happened. Careless workers inadvertently weakened the support for the huge pipe several days earlier during modification of the steel hangar to which it was attached at the McDonnell-Douglas plant in Long Beach. The accident did happen, however, and one consequence was that Richard Rodriguez was permanently paralyzed from the chest down and lost the use of one arm. But there was another consequence of the accident, as well, another life that was changed—. his wife's. And because of that other consequence, the status of women in California changed forever. No longer would a wife, legally, be the property of her husband.

The character and the essence of the rest of Richard Rodriguez's life had been changed because of someone else's negligence. Richard Rodriguez—once happy, healthy, and hopeful—now faced a grim lifetime as an invalid. He would have to be cared for during that lifetime. It would be expensive.

Richard Rodriguez, the law of California said, could be compensated for the damage done his life. He asked for general damages to compensate him for his life sentence to a wheelchair, plus reimbursement for past and future medical expenses, and compensation for the present loss of his earnings and his capacity for future earnings.

But Richard Rodriguez's life wasn't the only one changed by that falling pipe. Mary Anne Rodriguez was 20 years old, happily in love with her handsome, hard-working husband of 16 months when he went off to work on that fateful September day. She had a job of her own, and was helping to save for a home for the large family she and Richard planned to have. Life was joyful. Her future, like her husband's, was bright. But suddenly the character and the essence of her future were changed because of someone else's negligence.

Mary Anne Rodriguez—once happy, healthy, and hopeful—now faced a grim lifetime caring for her invalid husband. He couldn't dress himself. She would have to do it. He couldn't turn himself over in bed. She would have to do it. He couldn't empty his bladder or his bowels without help. She would have to provide that help.

For 24 hours of every day for the rest of her husband's life, she would have to be alert and responsive to his needs. She would never be able to choose a direction for her own life. She would never be able to hope her dreams would become a reality. She would never, ever, be her own person. She would never again share the joys of sex with her husband. She would never have his children.

But the law of California said Mary Anne Rodriguez could *not* be compensated for the damage done her life.

California law, like the laws of other states and the federal government, is based on English common law. And English common law on the issue Mary Anne Rodriguez and her Los Angeles lawyer, Ned Good, were addressing in 1974 was very clear. As articulated some 200 years ago by the eminent English jurist Sir William Blackstone, the common law held that "a wife could not recover for loss of her husband's services by the act of a third party for the starkly simple reason that she had no independent legal existence of her own and hence had no right to such services in the first place."

Ned Good was aware of the precedent when he filed his client's lawsuit, but he was determined to go forward nevertheless. Mary Anne Rodriguez's husband had been paralyzed in a preventable industrial accident, and she had been, in her attorney's words, "changed (from) a loving, vibrant young wife into a frustrated, unhappy, lonely nurse." Because of the accident to her husband, Good said, Mary Anne had suffered physical and emotional damages and was as deserving of compensation as Richard was. If existing law barred compensation, existing law should be changed. Had it been the wife who was paralyzed by an accident caused by negligence, the attorney argued, "California law gives the husband the right to sue for the loss of his wife's services." It was not proper or fair that a wife should be treated differently by the law.

As Good expected, the defendants petitioned the court to dismiss Mary Anne's complaint, "on the ground that no recovery for any such loss is permitted in California." Specifically, each of the defense briefs argued, "(A) wife is not, nor has she ever, been *entitled* to the services of her husband." A Superior Court judge reluctantly agreed, and dismissed her lawsuit.

But the law, fortunately, is a living entity. It changes, as society changes and as new judges bring new perspectives to old issues brought before them by determined lawyers.

And it changed for Mary Anne Rodriguez. It changed because a dedicated attorney believed in her cause and was willing, and financially able, to invest eight years of his time on the prospect of one day collecting a contingency fee.

Good not only had legal precedent going against him when he took on Mary Anne Rodriguez's case in addition to her husband's; he also faced an intimidating array of defense attorneys. McDonnell-Douglas was one defendant. Bethlehem Steel was another. Two other firms, Norman Engineering Co. and H.H. Robertson Co., were also named. Each had its own team of lawyers.

"It seemed like there were armies arrayed against us," Good recalled. "They had unlimited resources on their side. We had right on ours. Right won."

Early on, he says, he decided that although Richard and Mary Anne each had grounds for a lawsuit, they should merge their grievances into one suit with two separate causes of action, each claiming separate injuries caused by the accident.

"It was an absolutely tragic situation," Good said. "And Mary Anne was every bit as much a victim of the tragedy as Richard was. Richard would be compensated, there was no doubt. But I knew what the law was with respect to Mary Anne, and I knew that she was going to become a slave, in effect, economically as dependant on Richard as he was physically dependant on her. That just wasn't right, wasn't fair. And I believed then as I believe now, the law should be fair. The law should see that fairness is done." And so he began his long, tedious journey through the court system's appellate process.

While changes in the law do occur, they usually come, to borrow a phrase, exceeding slow. In 1930, a century and a half after Blackstone's *Commentaries*, Justice Isaac Isaacs of Australia's highest court dissented from a majority opinion, upholding the position stated by the English jurist.

A woman had sued "the other woman" for enticing her husband and persuading him to evict his wife from their home, "thereby disgracing her in the eyes of the world, separating her from her children, and even reducing her to poverty." Had the situation been reversed, Justice Isaacs wrote, the husband would have had an "unquestionable right to obtain redress for wrongful deprivation of consortium (based) on his right to physical possession of his wife, on which an action of trespass could be founded, and his property right in respect of her services in the quality of servant . . . ." The legal position that "there can be no analogous right in her to redress in the converse and precisely similar case . . . shock(s) the conscience," he continued.

Nevertheless, that was the position affirmed by a majority of the Australian court in 1930, and a quarter of a century later, most courts in the United States were no more enlightened. For instance, the Iowa Supreme Court ruled in 1956 that "at common law, the husband and wife were considered as one, and he was the one." And in 1958 and again in 1960, California's highest court had ruled that "a married person whose spouse has been injured by the negligence of a third party has no cause of action for loss of 'consortium,' (including) conjugal fellowship and sexual relations."

Despite the genderless language of the opinions, Mary Anne Rodriguez's lawyer argued, California men were able to recover when they lost the conjugal services of their wives because of a third party's negligence. But California wives could not even get into court if they lost the conjugal services of their husbands for the same reason.

"I go along with you, counsel, on your philosophy of the law, as to what the law ought to be," Long Beach Superior Court Judge Charles C. Stratton told Good at a hearing on the defense motion to dismiss Mary Anne's lawsuit, "(but) you say I can blaze a trail. I don't think trial judges are entitled to blaze trails."

Judge Stratton reluctantly granted the defendants' dismissal motion, which meant that no jury would have the opportunity to decide how much compensation Mary Anne was entitled to for the physical and emotional nightmare she was enduring and would continue to endure because of someone else's negligence.

That was not right, Good said. "There is no compelling reason of public policy to immunize a tortfeasor [wrongdoer] who changed a loving, vibrant young wife into a frustrated, unhappy, lonely nurse," he wrote in his passionate 23-page appeal of Judge Stratton's dismissal ruling. "A great portion of Mr. Rodriguez is medically dead," Good wrote. Mary Anne Rodriguez, consequently, "has all the burdens of widowhood without any of the legal rights of widowhood."

The law at the time was illogical as well as inequitable. Had Richard died as a consequence of the accident, Mary Anne *could* have recovered damages "for the loss of her deceased husband's society, comfort, and protection." But Richard did not die, and the defense lawyers argued that since a wife was in effect the "property" of her husband, if he were injured and received compensation, he was legally bound to use that compensation to continue the upkeep of his "property."

In addition to Mary Anne not being entitled, by law, to her husband's services, the defense argued, Mary Anne should not receive compensation because she was entitled by California's community property law to share in any compensation received by her husband. To compensate the husband for his injuries, and then to compensate the wife separately, would amount to a double recovery for the wife.

Suppose, Judge Stratton asked the defense attorneys, a husband earned $300 a month and his wife earned $500 a month. And suppose the husband was injured and had to give up his $300-a-month job. His wife had to give up her $500-a-month job to care for him.

Is it fair that the compensation be based only on the husband's salary?

That is the law, the defense lawyers said.

That is the law but it shouldn't be the law, Ned Good said.

That *was* the law, the Supreme Court said.

On Aug. 21, 1974, the California Supreme Court, with Justice Stanley Mosk writing the opinion for a 6-1 majority, reversed the lower court's dismissal of Mary Anne's lawsuit.

"After an exhaustive review," the decision's summary stated, "the Court held there was no significant support for the rule precluding a wife's recovery for loss of consortium caused by the husband's injury, rather than his death, in any of the arguments on which the decisions enforcing this rule rested.

"After noting that the rule was one of judicial creation and that the reasons for its existence had ceased, the Court abrogated it and declared that each spouse has a cause of action for loss of consortium caused by a negligent or intentional injury to the other by a third party."

The ruling in Mary Anne's case meant that California had finally caught up with much of the rest of the country on the equalizing of a husband's and wife's rights to receive compensation for damage done to their life by injuries inflicted on their spouse by a third party's negligence.

In 1958 only five states gave to wives the right to recover for loss of consortium. By 1974, when Ned Good was arguing the Rodriguez case before the California Supreme Court, 31 states held that view. The other 19, including California, either had not addressed the question or denied, either by statute or judicial ruling, the right of a wife to recover for loss of consortium. California was one of 13 which had established that denial by judicial ruling.

Good, in his appeal, cited the flowery language Michigan's Supreme Court had used when it voided the double standard in 1960: "The gist of the matter is that in today's society the wife's position is analogous to that of a partner, neither kitchen slattern nor upstairs maid," the opinion stated.

"Her duties and responsibilities in respect of the family unit complement those of the husband, extending only to another sphere. In the good times she lights the hearth with her own inimitable glow but when tragedy strikes it is a part of her unique glory that, forsaking shelter, the comfort, the warmth of the home, she puts her arm and shoulder to the plow.

"We are not at the heart of the issue. Such circumstances, when her husband's love is denied her, his strength sapped, and his protection destroyed, in short, when she has been forced by the defendant to exchange a heart for a husk, we are urged to rule that she has suffered no loss compensable at the law. But let some scoundrel dent a dishpan in the family kitchen and the law, in all its majesty, will convene the court, will march with measured tread to the halls of justice, and will there suffer a jury of her peers to assess the damages.

"Why are we asked, then, in the case before us to look the other way? Is this what is meant when it is said the justice is blind?"

Mosk kept his literary juices in check when he wrote the California court's opinion, but he made the same point. Citing the rulings in other states that had abandoned the medieval double standard, Mosk wrote that the historical legal basis for California's discriminatory law "has not only been undermined but destroyed. In its place a new common law has arisen, granting either spouse the right to recover for loss of consortium caused by negligent injury to the other spouse.

"Accordingly, to adopt that rule in California at this time (is) . . . a recognition of that liability as it is currently understood by the large preponderance of our sister states and a consensus of distinguished legal scholars."

The court's ruling meant that a trial would be held on Mary Anne Rodriguez's claim for compensation. Ned Good went ahead and tried the two cases together in a proceeding that lasted three months. The jury came in with its verdict on Feb. 9, 1976. Richard was awarded $4.1 million for his injuries, including compensation for the lifetime of medical care he would require. The jury awarded Mary Anne $500,000 for the damage done to her life. The $500,000 was an arbitrary amount, Good said, "but, remember, there was no precedent."

The ordeal wasn't over yet, however. The defendants appealed, and it wasn't until an appellate court upheld the jury verdicts on Dec. 21, 1978, and the Supreme Court declined on March 21, 1979, to rehear the appeal, that the process ended. Richard and Mary Anne Rodriguez finally collected their compensation. And Ned Good, after eight-plus years of litigation he describes as "long and tedious and difficult," finally collected a fee.

"I went to the Superior Court, then to the Court of Appeal, on to the Supreme Court, then back to the Superior Court for the three months of trial, back to the Appellate Court again when the defendants appealed the jury verdicts, and on to the Supreme Court again when the defendants petitioned for a rehearing," Good said. "I took 50, maybe 60 depositions. But what kept me going was that, as difficult as I thought it was for me, I could only imagine what life was like for Richard and Mary Anne. I'd have taken on that issue for free, I felt so strongly about it. I'd pay for the thrill of doing it again. It's what I became a lawyer for."

Of course during this long process there were lawyers for McDonnell-Douglas, Bethlehem Steel, and the other defendants who were doing what they were paid to do: everything possible to minimize the amount of damages their clients would have to pay.

The team of defense lawyers was certainly not philosophically committed to a world in which "the husband and wife were considered as one, and he was the one." They were simply doing all they could to minimize the compensation their clients would have to pay. And a law that treated women as property without rights, rather than as individuals with rights, obviously was valuable to that effort. The law as it existed saved their clients money, and so they became committed to the status quo.

The Rodriguez case graphically demonstrates a very basic reality underlying the current warfare over the shape and content of our civil law: While the goal of the law is to reflect society's agreed-upon values in a system of justice that is fair and responsive to the society it serves, there is money at stake here. Members of the defense lobby may agree piously with the abstract contention that a goal of the law is to reflect society's agreed-upon values, but when the concrete expression of one of those agreed-upon values—that people should be held financially responsible for damages they cause—costs or even threatens to cost them money, their actions suggest a different philosophy entirely.

That may be understandable—money has always been a powerful influence on philosophy—but it obviously is not acceptable. The rules of law, as they have developed throughout the decades, certainly give defendants every opportunity to challenge in court any claims that they are responsible for an injury, and to attempt to mitigate in court the cost to them if they are found to be responsible. However, too many members of the defense lobby are no longer interested in making their case in court, probably because they don't like what happens there.

Their answer instead is to try to prevent victims from being able to take their claims to court in the first place. Not persuade them, prevent them. The enormously powerful individuals and institutions who make up the defense lobby have demonstrated a willingness to invest whatever it takes to accomplish their objective, to change the laws to protect their bottom line. And that objective, regardless of the fancy language they use to disguise it, is to escape financial responsibility when they cause injury. Escape financial responsibility, and the bottom line—profits—is protected.

This is a dangerous situation. Members of the defense lobby are suppliers of products and services, many of them essential, and they are uniquely situated to cause serious harm when they act irresponsibly. Ford Motor Company makes billions of dollars selling us automobiles, but when it markets an automobile—the Pinto—that is little more than a rolling time bomb waiting for a tap on the bumper to explode, it has the capacity to cause death, horrible injury, and millions of dollars in damages to innocent consumers. Members of the children's clothing industry profit handily from our desire to keep our children warm and stylish, but they can cause unimaginable anguish when they market pajamas that burst into flames if they get too hot.

Professionals, whether doctors, lawyers, dentists, architects, or any others, enjoy a privileged status in our society and usually earn a reasonably comfortable income because we need their specialized training. But if they practice their profession in a negligent fashion, countless numbers of clients or patients can suffer serious damages at their hands.

In the past, because of unfair laws like the one the Rodriguez case changed, because of numerous procedural roadblocks that have only begun to be dismantled, and because of a conspiracy of silence that made it difficult if not impossible to get enough evidence to prove a case, these privileged institutions and professionals managed to escape responsibility for much of the harm they caused.

When the law began to change, as in the Rodriguez case, and when procedural roadblocks were dismantled and more and more courageous individuals broke the conspiracy of silence to speak up, the defense lobby became alarmed. Suddenly it was getting increasingly difficult to avoid responsibility for the real injuries it was causing.

In response we are seeing the defense lobby's skillfully

marketed nationwide campaign to turn the legal clock backwards; to, among other things, impose once again on Mary Anne Rodriguez and all other women their former legal status as mere chattels of their husbands. On March 21, 1979, Mary Anne Rodriguez led her California sisters into the 20th century. The "Beasts of Prey" have not come willingly with her.

3

LITIGATION EXPLOSION: THE BIG LIE

Obviously, the defense lobby's continuing use of the civil justice system as a battleground for its war on accountability would never receive much support from the public if it admitted to its real objective. From the start, the use of deception and the spreading of confusion have been essential elements in the campaign. Along with its use of the phrase "tort reform" (translation: Allow fewer victims to get their accusations of wrongdoing into court), it has invented a "litigation explosion" to justify the need for reform.

The insurance industry, one of the most powerful and committed members of the defense lobby, distributes through its Insurance Information Institute a booklet that asserts, "While our judicial system is basically a good one, it has been handicapped by unnecessary lawsuits . . . exorbitant awards, and unpredictable results." Chrysler Corporation President Lee Iacocca, in a 1987 speech to the American Bar Association, complained, "We're the most litigious society on earth. We sue each other at the drop of a hat."

(This grave concern for the health of our courts, by the way, was expressed by a man who knows about lawsuits. Lee Iacocca was executive vice president of the Ford Motor Company and the primary moving force behind the firm's development of the Pinto in 1968. He still held that position in 1972 when the firm decided to save money by not eliminating design defects, discovered by its safety engineers, that increased the vulnerability of the Pinto's gas tank to rupture during a collision.)

Lawsuits, the theme articulated by Iacocca and others goes, are proliferating faster than fruit flies. There are so many being filed by greedy "victims" and even greedier lawyers that they're clogging the system and preventing legitimate lawsuits from being heard. A legitimate lawsuit, of course, is defined as one filed by a corporation or corporate executive seeking compensation for a wrong allegedly done. Pennzoil's lawsuit against Texaco was a "legitimate lawsuit" under this definition. Not only is there a prodigious proliferation of greed-motivated lawsuits filed by undeserving plaintiffs, the campaign theme contends, but wacky, out-of-control juries are giving huge, unjustified awards to plaintiffs.

Aiding the defense lobby's campaign is the media's slavish devotion to the sensational. No newspaper, for example, is going to put a headline reading "MOTHER TERESA WALKS OFF WITH $200,000" over a story about a donation to her charitable work, but exactly that kind of journalism appears regularly in coverage of the civil justice system. Headlines like: "WOMAN WINS $200,000 FOR SLIP ON BANANA PEEL" appear frequently, usually with little or no explanation of what actually happened or what the woman's real injuries were. And the articles never mention the fact that a jury of 12 citizens actually sat through an entire trial, learned exactly what had happened, knew who was at fault, knew what the real extent of injuries was, and, after hearing all the arguments and evidence on both sides of the issue, rendered its verdict.

The sowing of confusion has been an effective campaign tactic. People don't know much about what the civil justice system is or how it operates, and don't really want to know. As I pointed out in the Preface, it is a system our instincts tell us we should avoid. So, when we hear about the "litigation explosion" and the claims about excessive jury verdicts, over and over again, eventually the constant combination of distortion and slander by anecdote becomes accepted as fact. Furthermore, the only people who can respond to the wild charges in a timely manner with accurate information are lawyers, and we all know nobody will pay any attention to what they say.

The allegations of a litigation explosion and wacky give-the-store-away juries, however, are serious and, if we are to assume the best of intentions for the moment, urgent. Obviously, if the system of civil justice is really spiraling out of control, something needs to be done.

Is there a litigation explosion or isn't there? After all, if things are as bad as the defense lobby claims, a rapidly increasing number of lawsuits should be relatively easy to prove. Are juries really giving away the store? Well, there have been studies, many of them, on both subjects, and the simple fact is all relevant statistical data demonstrates clearly that there has been neither an explosion in litigation nor a tendency on the part of jurors to hand out awards in excess of proven damages.

Assertions of a litigation explosion are simply unfounded, and there has been no analytical evidence supporting the existence of an "explosion" in either the number of lawsuits filed or the size of the claims paid. The issues have been studied carefully by sources as diverse as the Rand Corporation, the National Association of Attorneys General, the National Center for State Courts, numerous academic researchers, the United States General Accounting Office, and even *Business Week* magazine. All have concluded the litigation explosion is a myth, and that the vast majority of jury verdicts have remained stable over time.

The United States General Accounting Office looked into the "litigation explosion" assertion in 1988 and produced a report to the House of Representatives Subcommittee on Commerce, Consumer Protection, and Competitiveness. It stated that between 1974 and 1986 there was indeed a substantial increase of tort filings in the federal courts. "We found, however," the report states, "that a significant part of the growth (75 percent) is concentrated in one product, asbestos."

Product liability filings unrelated to asbestos and two other products with recently discovered problems, the Dalkon Shield contraceptive device and Bendectin, a morning-sickness drug, "have grown at about the same rate as civil filings in general and personal expenditures on goods," the report stated, adding: "These data seem inconsistent with the contention that there is a rapidly accelerating growth in federal product liability filings across a wide range of products."

The mild increase in product liability lawsuits filed in federal courts involving "products in general," the report concluded, "appears to be neither rapidly accelerating nor explosive."

Even the fact that courts were being inundated with asbestos-related lawsuits was twisted to serve the campaign's purpose, an illustration of the cleverness and determination of the defense lobby's campaign. Manufacturers and their industrial clients destroyed the lives of hundreds of thousands of innocent people by knowingly exposing them to dangerous levels of asbestos, keeping a tight conspiracy of silence for over 30 years about the deadly effects those fibers were having on people's lungs. Then, when the disease finally began to manifest itself in a deadly procession of victims, the very corporations that created the tragedy in the first place denied liability and forced each and every victim to file a separate lawsuit. The manufacturers—and the other members of the defense lobby—then attempted to use the huge number of lawsuits as evidence of a justice system out of control.

In 1986 the Insurance Information Institute began to actively promote the assertion that there had been a "sixfold increase" in civil lawsuits in federal court from 1940 to the early 1980s, offering that statistic as strong evidence of the "litigation explosion." University of Wisconsin law professor Marc Galanter acknowledged in a study that there had indeed been a substantial increase in all civil litigation in federal courts. But, he concluded from his examination of civil filings from 1960 through 1986, legal disputes between businesses made the largest contribution to the 398 percent increase during those 26 years. Contract disputes increased by 258 percent, far outstripping the 114 percent growth of personal injury and property damage filings, Galanter said, and by 1986 were the largest category of civil filings in the federal courts.

In a later study, "Reading the Landscape of Disputes," which appeared in the *UCLA Law Review*, Galanter added that the most recent increase in federal lawsuits resulted first from the Reagan administration's attempt to collect "over-payments" in veterans' loans and Social Security payments or to collect on defaulted student loans; and second, from claims brought by individuals attempting to restore disability payments cut off by the administration.

Although the General Accounting Office report mentioned earlier noted a trend toward filing product liability lawsuits in federal courts rather than state courts, the percentage filed in federal court is still so small that the GAO findings should not be assumed to reflect similar conclusions about state court filings, the House subcommittee was told.

Fine. Let's look at studies of state court filings, which account for 98 percent of all tort actions in the country. According to *A Preliminary Examination of Available Civil and Criminal Trend Data in State Trial Courts for 1978, 1981, and 1984,* compiled in 1986 by Robert Roper of the National Center for State Courts, ". . . total tort filings (for those years) increased 9 percent; however, the population also increased by 9 percent. This does not qualify as a 'litigation explosion.'"

The report acknowledged that court statistics in all 50 states were not included because not every state accumulated the statistical information the project required. Its findings were based on statistics from the 21 court systems that were examined, it explained. In California during that period, tort filings (including product liability lawsuits) increased 12 percent, the same increase as the state's population. In Florida, while the population was increasing by 20 percent, tort filings increased by only 13 percent. New York reported no population increase, but a tort filing increase of six percent over the six-year period.

Separate studies reported in the Spring 1985 issue of *Judges Journal*, exploring the history of civil filings in the state of Illinois, and in the June 1985 issue of *Law, Medicine, and Health Care*, drew similar conclusions also demonstrating the myth of the "litigation explosion."

These findings concur with the conclusion the Rand Corporation drew in its study, *Trends in Tort Litigation*. After reviewing the State Court data and its own comparable estimates, Rand concluded, "Whatever the slight difference among estimates, it is clear that the amount of tort litigation nationwide is growing relatively slowly. Indeed, when the rate is adjusted for population growth, it sinks to a modest three percent."

Perhaps the most comprehensive and thoughtful examination of litigation rates in the United States has been done by Professor Galanter. Galanter notes that rates of litigation fluctuate over time, with the number of lawsuits per capita peaking at different times over our history. Peaks were reached in the 1820s, 1890s, and the 1920s, Galanter says, adding that on the whole, the fluctuations have been minimal. Galanter also found that, contrary to Lee Iacocca's assertion, the litigious nature of the American people is approximately the same as that of the citizens of Australia, New Zealand, England, Denmark, and Israel.

So much for a litigation explosion. What about skyrocketing jury verdicts?

More than 30 years ago, the University of Chicago conducted a study of jury verdicts and concluded, "The fears voiced by critics that jurors are led by bias, incompetence, and irrelevant facts to make capricious decisions are not substantiated."

The Rand Corporation, which has collected the most reliable recent long-term data on jury verdicts, agrees. Rand studied extensive jury verdict information from both San Francisco County in California and Cook County in Illinois over a 24-year period from 1960 through 1984. Rand's conclusion: "Our research shows that jurors are usually sensible, and that their decisions have been remarkably stable over 20 years."

When Rand broke the tort cases down into subcategories, the figures did demonstrate a noticeable increase in jury awards over the past 20 years in both product liability and medical malpractice cases. However, the reason for the increase in those kinds of cases had nothing to do with out-of-control juries and everything to do with the dramatic increases in the cost of medical care, Rand concluded.

Product liability and medical malpractice cases tend to involve the most seriously injured victims, often those with catastrophic injuries. Both the medical costs of caring for these people and the economic losses caused by such injuries are increasing significantly faster than inflation. Indeed, another Rand Corporation study, *Compensation of Injuries*, found the medical cost component of verdicts for seriously injured people had increased nearly 200 percent over a nine-year period.

The same study concluded, "It seems likely that medical advances in treating catastrophic injuries might have contributed to the increasing size of the largest awards—partly because the medical advances were more expensive. Also, these advances may have increased the survival rate for persons with catastrophic injuries while often leaving them with severe handicaps that require continuing medical custodial care."

Despite the overwhelming evidence to the contrary, the wagers of the war continue to scream "litigation explosion" and "out-of-control juries," and get away with it. They are able to do that because they're using the most sophisticated of modern marketing techniques in their effort to convince consumers that "reforms" are needed in the civil justice system. We've gone from marketing products to marketing candidates and now to marketing political agendas, and in the marketing world "truth" is not nearly as important as "believability" and "perception." It had to be someone in the marketing world who prompted the observation that "perception is reality."

As in any good marketing scheme, the goal is instant message penetration and the defense lobby's message, to help justify its "tort reform" objective, is "litigation explosion." The lobby was able to employ modern marketing skills when the United States Attorney General's office released a report ostensibly discussing the causes and extent of insurance problems that were then sweeping the country. One of its main conclusions was that "the growth in the number of product liability suits has been astounding. For example, the number of product liability cases filed in federal district courts has increased from 1,579 in 1974 to 13,554 in 1985, a 758 percent increase.... There is no reason to believe that the state courts have not witnessed a similar dramatic increase in the number of product liability claims."

In fact as we have already seen, state courts have not witnessed anything like the reported increase in federal filings (which, remember, were skewed by the huge number of asbestos cases), particularly since the National Center for State Courts

47

determined state court tort filings (accounting for 95 percent of all tort actions in this country) have essentially tracked population growth.

The defense lobby's campaign managers also made creative use of selected statistics to buttress the attack on another cherished aspect of the civil justice, the jury. The country was told repeatedly of findings by the U.S. Attorney General's office that "the average product liability jury award in 1984 was $1.07 million, and the average medical malpractice award was $850,000." The years and numbers changed from time to time in different published articles and speeches, but the overall purpose was always the same, to shock people into believing that juries across the country were handing out vast sums of money on a daily basis.

The problem, however, is that the "statistics" were totally meaningless. The source for the data was Jury Verdict Research (JVR) of Solon, OH, a jury verdict reporting service with a very unscientific manner of collecting information. Not only does JVR not purport to collect all or even most of the verdicts in the country (in 1984 JVR reported on only 238 medical malpractice cases in the entire country), but its methods of collection guarantee that it will report only a small number of the very highest verdicts.

Most of the verdicts reported, JVR acknowledged, came either from newspaper clippings or from the attorneys themselves. Obviously only the large cases tend to be reported by the press, and not many attorneys are going to write in to report a small jury verdict. Nevertheless, JVR offered what it claimed was "data" supporting conclusions about "average" jury awards. Additionally, the "averages" did not include verdicts for the defense (which wins more than 50 percent of the time); they did not include settlements (which are almost always considerably less than jury verdicts); and they were not adjusted to reflect reductions of the jury award by either the trial court or the appellate court. In short, the figures were completely meaningless except to indicate that both poorly designed products and medical negligence routinely cause some absolutely catastrophic injuries.

What made the entire charade such a travesty was the purposeful deception. Some weeks after his national press conference to publicize the frightening "averages," Assistant United States Attorney General Richard K. Willard gave testimony on them before the Senate Commerce Committee's Subcommittee on Consumer Affairs, and was questioned by Senator Ernest F. Hollings of South Carolina:

Hollings: "Well, how do they (JVR) gather it? That is what I'm asking."

Willard: "They gather it from people who write in and report it to them, from newspapers clippings, from a variety of services."

Hollings: "Come on now, you are an Attorney General. You are not going to come up and testify about newspaper clippings."

Willard: "Well, Senator, we do not use Jury Verdict Research, Inc., statistics as being accurate as to absolute data, as to average jury verdicts."

But Willard and the managers of the defense lobby's slick campaign against the civil justice system have no hesitation in using the "statistics" to suit their purpose. I call that fraud, and a dangerously deceitful one at that.

The academics use kinder words, but no less damning. As Professor Galanter said in concluding his impressive analysis of over two centuries worth of information on litigation in the United States, "We have seen the announcement of general conclusions relevant to policy on the basis of very casual scholarly activity. The information base was thin and spotty; theories were put forward without serious examination of whether they fit the facts; values and preconceptions were left unarticulated. Portentous pronouncements were made by established dignitaries and publicists in learned journals. Could one imagine public health specialists or poultry breeders conjuring up epidemics and cures with such cavalier disregard of the incompleteness of the data and the untested nature of the theory?"

The answer, of course, is "No," but this is no ordinary policy debate. For the defense lobby, this is war, and nothing matters but winning.

4

THE KING
CAN DO WRONG

The Yuba and Feather Rivers come together some 50 miles north of Sacramento in Northern California and, like rivers everywhere, can turn from gentle flows to raging torrents in heavy rain storms. A series of levees protect nearby property owners, but during a particularly heavy storm in 1955, one levee proved inadequate and much of Sutter County was flooded. Devastated residents were not pleased to learn that the state flood control district responsible for the levee had not designed it to handle the merging rivers at their predictable peak flow.

Had the defective levee been designed and built by a private firm there would have been a clear responsibility to the flood-soaked homeowners. The levee's designers and builders worked for the government, however, and the law of the time insulated their employers from lawsuits. The property owners could have sued the government if the government agreed to be sued, or they could have

51

sued had the law specifically allowed the kind of suit they wanted to file. Neither circumstance pertained in 1955. Nevertheless, 160 of the property owners retained the law firm of Goldstein, Barceloux, and Goldstein from Chico, the nearest big town, to seek compensation for the damage caused by the flood that never should have happened.

The outraged homeowners succeeded, eventually, because three years later, Louisa Muskopf was dropped on the floor by some careless attendants in a Northern California hospital and re-injured the broken hip for which she was being treated.

The law works like that, sometimes. A legal concept is introduced, developed, refined over time, and sometimes, adopted in a matter seemingly unrelated to the original one. That's what happened in Louisa Muskopf's situation. She was able to have her lawsuit heard because a stubborn lawyer had persisted in arguing a novel concept to the state's judges: The king *can* do wrong. And be sued if he does. And because she won the right to have her lawsuit heard, the Sutter County property owners also won that right.

It may seem difficult to believe today, but less than three decades ago most of our country's citizens did not have the general right to sue their government. Californians have that right now, and the Supreme Court decision that gave them that right did not involve a multimillion-dollar dispute, the kind that attracts big headlines in a newspaper. It involved an average sort of case, the kind that occupies most of the time of trial lawyers specializing in personal injury lawsuits.

Louisa Muskopf was being treated in Corning Memorial Hospital for a broken hip, and while she was being moved between a bed and a gurney, she was dropped. On the floor. On her hip. She was hurting, and she was angry. The attendants, she thought, had simply been careless. Sorry didn't cover it. Not when it meant she hurt more, longer, and had to stay in the hospital for an additional period. She sued.

Sue away, said hospital officials. We are a part of the Corning Hospital District, which is a state governmental entity. A government, even a subunit of government, can't be sued unless the law specifically allows it. There was no exception to the rule for hospital districts.

Louisa Muskopf asked for $25,000 as compensation for the injury and pain caused by the carelessness of the hospital's employees. Her suit was finally settled out of court in 1964, three years after the Supreme Court decision, with the amount of the settlement not disclosed publicly. But that court decision in Louisa Muskopf's relatively small-potatoes case enabled landowners in Sutter County to hold the government accountable for negligence that resulted in the devastation of their property.

Attorney Reginald M. Watt handled both cases for the Chico law firm. He knew what the legal precedent was: The government had "sovereign immunity," a holdover from the feudal concept that "the king can do no wrong." Although numerous exceptions to that general rule had crept into the law over time, the doctrine itself still ruled throughout most of the country and had not been seriously challenged. None of the exceptions would have permitted the property owners to get their case in court. And, as noted, the governments declined to let themselves be sued.

"When I was preparing for the flood cases, I spent a year and a half reading every single sovereign immunity case that had ever been tried in the United States, Canada, and England," Watt recalls. "I was convinced that the doctrine was erroneous to begin with, had become part of the common law by mistake, and had been picked up in our law for no reason that made any sense." He decided to challenge the rule.

"I didn't want to use the flood cases to challenge the rule, because many of the property owners had been utterly devastated by the flood and if we failed, there would be no second chance. They would have been ruined," Watt recalls. "But there were plenty of other opportunities to get the issue before the Supreme Court, and I tried seven different times to have the sovereign immunity rule reconsidered. The first three times I took a Superior Court judge's dismissal of a case to the Supreme Court, not one justice voted to hear it. Then I got one vote, then two, then two again. Then I took up the Muskopf case, on the same point, and five (of the seven) justices voted to consider it." Watt, retained originally by the flood-devastated Sutter County property owners, used the Muskopf case to overturn the sovereign immunity rule.

Roger Traynor, who later became the chief justice of the California Supreme Court and one of the most respected jurists in this country's history, wrote the ruling reversing the lower court dismissal of Louisa Muskopf's lawsuit. He made it clear that the 5-2 majority was fully aware of the enormity of its decision. Early in the Jan. 27, 1961, opinion he says simply, "After a re-evaluation of the rule of governmental immunity from tort liability we have concluded that it must be discarded as mistaken and unjust."

A tort is a wrongful act, either negligent or intentional, by one person or entity against another. It did not become less wrongful by virtue of having been committed by a governmental entity. The Supreme Court was discarding a rule of common law that had existed in England for more than four centuries and had been picked up by state courts when the United States was an infant nation.

The rule of sovereign immunity, Traynor wrote, began in feudal times. No lord of a manor could be sued in a court under his authority, and similarly, the king could not be sued by any court because no court was above him. It was unclear how the immunity claimed by kings came to be conferred on government, and Traynor quotes an early American legal writer who stated the exportation of the concept from England to the United States is "one of the mysteries of legal evolution."

It was particularly strange, Watt argued 29 years ago,

because the whole notion of "sovereign immunity" was foreign to the basic philosophy of the early Americans: The government is the servant of the people, not the other way around. In addition, the specific Massachusetts case in which the concept was first used in the United States differed substantially from the seminal English case, *Russell v. Men of Devon*, which was cited in the Massachusetts ruling, Traynor says, suggesting strongly that in his view the linkage was unsound.

Nevertheless, the concept was judicially recognized, eventually even in California. Despite the fact that sovereign immunity became "riddled with exceptions," Traynor wrote, the basic concept remained.

"The rule of governmental immunity from tort is an anachronism, without rational basis, and has existed only by the force of inertia. None of the reasons for its continuance can withstand analysis. No one defends governmental immunity. In fact, it does not exist. It has become riddled with exceptions, both legislative and judicial, and the exceptions operate so illogically as to cause serious inequality," he said.

"Some who are injured by governmental agencies can recover, others cannot; one injured while attending a community theater in a public park may recover, but one injured in a children's playground may not.

"The illogical and inequitable extreme is reached in this case: We are asked to affirm a rule that denies recovery to one injured in a county or hospital *district* hospital, although recovery may be had by one injured in a city and county hospital."

Justice Traynor methodically worked through the pro and con arguments, including the position by Federal Appeals Court Justice Learned Hand that it is "better to leave unredressed the wrongs done by dishonest (government) officers than to subject those who try to do their duty to the constant dread of retaliation."

The practical reality, Traynor wrote, is that so many exceptions have become part of the law that "(o)nly the vestigial remains of . . . governmental immunity have survived; its requiem has long been foreshadowed. For years the process of erosion of governmental immunity has gone on unabated. The Legislature has contributed mightily to that erosion. The courts, by distinction and extension, have removed much of the force of the rule.

"Thus, in holding that the doctrine of governmental immunity for torts for which its agents are liable has no place in our law we make no startling break with the past but merely take the final step that carries to its conclusion an established legislative and judicial trend."

Even if Louisa Muskopf had not been dropped on her already-broken hip, Justice Traynor implied, the doctrine of sovereign immunity in California would eventually have been discarded anyway. But it was discarded when it was discarded, in January of 1961, because a small-town attorney believed the doctrine was wrong and kept pressing that belief with lawsuit after lawsuit and appeal after appeal until he forced the California Supreme Court to re-evaluate it.

Each of the seven cases in which the sovereign immunity rule was challenged by Reg Watt was handled on a contingency fee basis: no payment for the lawyer unless success is achieved. Six times Reg Watt researched extensively and prepared diligently to bring the sovereign immunity rule before the state Supreme Court so the firm's client at the time could bring a grievance against a government into court. Six times he and his client lost. Six times the client did not recover from the governmental agency that had allowed an injury to occur. Six times the plaintiffs' counsels made not a dime for their effort.

"I didn't really make any money even from the Muskopf case," Watt said. "I handled the appeal, and when we won that another lawyer handled it afterward. What motivated me during those years before we finally got into court was indignation, as much as anything else. The very idea that there was a question about whether a government had a responsibility to act with reasonable care seemed incredible to me. Thankfully, the law has the capacity to change. It is still changing. It's not always right—in the 1850s the California Supreme Court, in *People v. Hall*, held that Chinese persons could not testify in court—but it has the capacity to change its mind, to right a wrong. Some decisions coming down today will be looked on with horror 140 years from now, as we look with horror on the Hall decision. Those decisions will change because some lawyer got indignant enough, and was financially able, to keep bringing the issue before the court."

Reg Watt spent ten years researching and arguing the sovereign immunity issue before he and his 160 Sutter County property owner clients finally, in 1965, won a $6.3 million judgment from the governmental entities they could not have taken into court in the first place without those ten years of research and preparation by their lawyer. Reg Watt finally collected a fee in a sovereign immunity case, earning a place in California's legal history because his fee was the *last* fee collected in a sovereign immunity case. The law, the ever-evolving law, had changed, continuing a process that has existed since mankind first began seeking a non-violent method of settling disputes.

"Even when laws are written down," Aristotle wrote nearly 2,400 years ago, "they ought not always to remain unaltered."

And, of course, few do. Even some of the ten simple, straightforward laws Moses brought down from the mountain have "evolved" over time into something other than their original meaning. "Thou shalt not kill," for instance, would appear in today's law books as "Thou shalt not kill, except in circumstances approved by society such as war, self-defense, and capital punishment . . . . "

The ability to change is what gives law its strength. Frederic W. Maitland, a 19th century English legal scholar, wrote that ". . . a body of law . . . (is) a being that lives and grows, that preserves its identity while every atom of which it is composed is subject to a ceaseless process of change, decay, and renewal."

Shakespeare had something to say about that which is particularly pertinent here. Lord Angelo, one of his principal characters in *Measure for Measure*, begins Act II by advising that

We must not make a scarecrow of the law,
Setting it up to fear the birds of prey,
And let it keep one shape, till custom make it
Their perch and not their terror.

The law has changed, is changing, and will continue to change. I'm not going to presume to try, in these few pages, to present a comprehensive history of the law. It is amazing, though, as Maitland said, how "identity" is preserved despite change, how often connections can be found between the underpinnings of the laws of today and those of their antecedents.

It is probable, for instance, that every commencement speech ever given, or going to be given, to a class of graduating law school seniors implores the graduates, hopefully in less stilted language, "to make justice to appear in the land, to destroy the evil and the wicked that the strong might not oppress the weak...." The thought is not original, but speakers need not be embarrassed. The thought likely was not original even 40 centuries ago when it was used by Hammurabi as an introduction to his code of laws, imposed on the people of Babylon in 2100 B.C. in one of the earliest examples of written law.

The English translation of the Code of Hammurabi consists of the introduction plus 65 paragraphs of laws and punishments. Many of the laws are articulations of themes still found in our laws today: Protect the weak from the strong; hold people (including businesses and governments) accountable if they do wrong; have the wrongdoer compensate the person he or she has injured. The punishments imposed by the Code of Hammurabi were generally far harsher than those prescribed by our laws of today, but were then as they are now a response to activities considered harmful to a healthy society.

Look at some of the punishments called for by Hammurabi. A man accusing another of manslaughter, but unable to prove the accusation, "shall be put to death," he wrote. "If a fire has broken out in a man's house and a man who has gone to extinguish (it) has coveted an article of the owner of the house and takes the article of the owner of the house, that man shall be cast into the fire," the code reads. Another: "If a man has broken into a house, they shall put him to death and hang him before the breach which he has made." There is punishment for judges who make a decision and then change their minds, and punishment for officers of the king who abuse their authority.

There are laws governing business dealings, including one that today's farmers might like to see enacted. Bankers—money-lenders—were undoubtedly as powerful in ancient Babylon as they are today, but Hammurabi's code nevertheless states, "If a man incurs a debt and Adad (a god) inundates his field or a flood has carried away (the soil) or else (if) corn is not raised on the field through lack of water, in that year he shall not render (any) corn to (his) creditor; he shall not pay interest for that year."

The Code of Hammurabi, Greek law, Roman law, the Koran, the Talmud, the Bible, and the Magna Charta all were among the influences—some direct, some indirect—on the English common law, and it is the English common law that is the rock upon which most of our judicial rulings rest today.

Section 22.2 of California's Civil Code spells out the relationship: "The Common Law of England, so far as it is not repugnant to or inconsistent with the Constitution of the United States or the Constitution or the laws of this state, is the rule of decision in all the courts of this state."

Another section of the Civil Code, 325.3, states, "For every wrong, there is a remedy," and sometimes the two provisions conflict. There was a conflict with respect to the status of women, and when it was finally resolved the law of California was quite different from the common law. The king could do no wrong under common law, but California law now recognizes that he (government) can, and must compensate the victim when he does.

Sometimes the law does decay and take a step backward. Sometimes it is simply abused. The book *Treasury of Law*, from which the Hammurabi references were taken, quotes one Dagobert D. Runes who says, "Looking back at antiquity, the Dark Ages, the Feudal Era, or even observing modern times, one shudders not at what people did unlawfully, but rather at what crimes were committed in the name of the law."

That still occurs, sadly, and may continue to occur, always. But what we have now that didn't always exist is the mechanism for remedying even a legal wrong—or, at least, having a legal action believed wrong re-examined.

Our appellate process is one of the evidences that the law has refined itself and grown stronger during the past 4,000 years and is still renewing and refining itself and growing yet stronger. It is not perfect, but in the civil law the weak do have more protection from the strong than they had a decade or a century or 40 centuries ago; and more accountability has been imposed on individuals, governments, businesses, doctors, and hospitals—and, yes, on lawyers.

Sometimes the changes occur because of enlightened legislatures, sometimes because of enlightened justices who let new issues be tried before juries.

For justices to have the opportunity to let new law develop, they have to have the appropriate issue presented to them. In the civil law, it is usually a trial lawyer, often working for a contingency fee, who brings an issue to the court, sometimes over and over again, until a court determines the legal precedent being challenged should be re-examined. The opportunity to right a wrong, to make justice be done, is one incentive motivating trial lawyers, but certainly the opportunity to collect a fee is another, and the possibility that a jury might impose punitive damages—an award to the plaintiff when the defendant has acted with callous disregard for safety—from which the lawyer would collect a still larger fee, is an inducement to take on a complex, time-consuming case.

The continuing attacks on the civil justice system are aimed at discouraging lawyers from taking those complex, time-consuming cases, the kind that can result in large judgments. A consequence of that is victims are denied the ability to bring issues involving accountability to court. Had the ability to bring issues to court not existed in the past, had the strong retained the legal ability they once had to protect themselves from the weak, the law would not have changed; certainly, it would not have changed to the extent it has.

To sum up: the law was meant to change; it is strong because it can change; it is changing, generally for the better; and it is changing, in part, because lawsuits are brought before judges and juries. That process must not be altered, nor must the purpose of the law, "to make justice to appear in the land, to destroy the evil and the wicked that the strong might not oppress the weak," be rewritten to serve the interests only of the strong!

5

THE KEY
TO THE COURTHOUSE

Insurance companies don't like it when policyholders make claims, and they don't like it when they get taken to court for refusing to pay claims, and they don't like it when juries hold them accountable, and they don't like it when they not only have to pay the claims they should have paid in the first place but a big chunk of punitive damages as well.

There are a lot of things insurance companies don't like, but probably what they don't like most is the contingency fee system that allows all those other things they don't like to happen.

The phrase "contingency fee" doesn't explain clearly enough what occurs when a trial lawyer agrees to represent a client without a fee unless the client receives compensation from the defendant. A more accurate phrase is "result fee." If the result is good for the client, the lawyer gets paid. If the result is not good, the lawyer does not get paid. Eventually, perhaps, the phrase "result fee" will come into use, but until then, I'll continue to use the old, more familiar terminology to describe the practice that insurance companies don't like.

Many manufacturers and retailers and providers of services, including doctors and hospitals, don't like the contingency fee system either. It provides access to the nation's legal system for consumers who complain that a product or a service is not as advertised and has caused them physical or emotional or economic injury, and for employees who claim an injury occurred because they had to work with unsafe equipment or under unsafe conditions. And once a complaint is in the American civil justice system, the enormous economic advantage big business has over the consumer or employee who made it is neutralized.

That puts a 20-year-old unemployed woman with a paralyzed husband on even legal footing with the McDonnell-Douglas and Bethlehem Steel companies, and gives anyone else who has been made a victim—regardless of wealth or education or even ability to speak the English language—just as much power and authority and ability to influence a jury inside a courtroom as the government of the state of California or the Ford Motor Company or a wealthy and powerful insurance company.

Insurance companies, manufacturers, retailers, providers of services and, sometimes even governments, don't like being only equal. It takes away the edge their financial advantage gives them, and they like their edge.

As it stands now, the process is there for anybody to use, and would be there even if there were no contingency fee. But that's like saying there's a nice fancy courthouse available for your use, but it's locked and there's no key. The contingency fee system provides the key to the courthouse in the civil justice system. Without the key, entry into the courthouse, for all practical purposes, is denied to less-than-wealthy people who feel they are not being treated fairly by an insurance company, manufacturer and seller of a product, or provider of a service.

And that statement, by the way, is not coming from a trial lawyer worried about his income. The Rand Corporation studied contingency fees for the U.S. Department of Health, Education, and Welfare, and in June of 1980 produced a report concluding: "Ceilings on the contingency fee percentage may significantly reduce the number of hours an attorney will spend on a case and effectively bar certain cases from trial." Such a restriction, the report continued, could be expected to "deter . . . low and middle-income plaintiffs from filing even meritorious suits."

Very simply, Mary Anne Rodriguez and Louisa Muskopf might never have gotten into court in the first place had they not been able to enter into a contingency fee contract with a personal injury lawyer; and, given the caliber of the defendants' ample and able counsel, they might very well have lost their cases had they not been able to sign those contracts with *experienced* personal injury lawyers.

Only a very small percentage—less than ten percent—of all lawyers devote a majority of their practice to personal injury law and work for contingency fees, and despite the claims to the contrary, they aren't with the biggest, wealthiest firms. Of the 50 largest law firms in California, none is a plaintiffs' personal injury firm, and never in California history has a law firm primarily working for result fees ever cracked the top 50.

Most lawyers do the kind of work that requires a client to sign a binding commitment to pay either a flat fee or an hourly fee plus expenses (for however many hours the case requires); or they work on salary for a single employer, the government, say, or an insurance company or some other corporation. You want a will, you go to a lawyer in private practice, tell him or her what you want, you're told what it will cost, and if you agree to the amount the lawyer prepares your will and sends you a bill. Same with obtaining an uncontested divorce, having a business partnership agreement drafted, or the hundreds of other kinds of fairly simple legal needs that require the preparation of a binding document.

There are other legal needs that are not simple, however, and a lawyer may charge an hourly fee instead. The more complex the legal need—resolution of a contested divorce or other dispute, for instance—the more time required to settle the issue in controversy, the larger the lawyer's fee. A wealthy person obviously would have no difficulty finding a lawyer to represent him or her in just about any kind of a legal matter, including suing some other individual or a business believed to have caused the injury.

But let's look at a person who is not wealthy and is being treated unfairly by someone who is wealthy and powerful and arrogant. Let's look at U.L. Fletcher, a Southern California manual laborer.

At work one day at his warehouse job, U.L. Fletcher tried to move a 361-pound bale of rubber. He hurt himself, badly enough that he had to stop work and see a doctor, who told him he wasn't going to go back to his job for awhile. It was January 1965. Fletcher was 41 years old. He had quit school after the fourth grade and been a laborer all his working life. At the time of his injury, he had been working an average of 70 to 80 hours a week so he could earn $289 to take care of his wife and eight children. Seven of his eight children were in school. Being unable to work because of the injuries could have been devastating to his family, but, fortunately, Fletcher had planned well. Two years earlier, he had purchased a disability insurance policy from Western National Life Insurance Company. He had paid his premiums faithfully, and he was covered.

He thought.

Western National paid the $150-a-month benefit called for by the policy during the six months Fletcher spent recovering from a hernia operation and other problems diagnosed after his injury. When he tried going back to work, however, he found he couldn't do the heavy labor required. He was laid off.

Fletcher's own physician and several physicians handling worker's compensation cases examined him and declared him to have a work-related disability. Under the terms of his policy, Western National was obligated to pay him $150 monthly for 30 years if the disability was caused by an injury. That would be a total of $54,000. If, however, the disability was caused by an illness, the $150 a month would be paid for only two years. That would total $3,600, a difference to Western National of $50,400.

The difference was apparently enough for Western National to ignore the doctors' diagnoses and inform Fletcher that his disability was illness-related and that consequently his benefits would cease after two years. Not content with that, the firm subsequently notified Fletcher that, in its opinion, his back problem resulted from a congenital defect he had failed to tell the company about when he took out the policy. So, since he would never have been insured in the first place had the congenital problem been disclosed, he would have to reimburse to the firm the $2,038 in benefits he had already received. Out of the kindness of the firm's heart, Fletcher was informed, Western National would forgive the $2,038 if he signed a document agreeing not to contest its decision to cancel the policy and pay him no additional benefits.

Not much imagination is need to comprehend U.L. Fletcher's predicament: U.L. Fletcher, no money, no education, up against Western National Life Insurance Co., big company, lots of money, big-time lawyers. No contest.

Well, there *was* a contest. Fletcher, who had had the good sense to take out a disability insurance policy in the first place, also had the good sense to look for a lawyer when he felt his insurance company was trying to stiff him. Eventually he wound up with Arthur N. Hews of Santa Ana, California, a trial lawyer who specialized in personal injury cases. Hews listened, did some checking, and agreed to represent Fletcher. The attorney took the case on contingency, meaning he would receive a percentage of any award Fletcher received. If Western National won, if Fletcher received nothing, Arthur Hews would also receive nothing.

Hews filed a complaint containing three counts. The first asked that Western National be ordered to pay the $150 monthly benefit for the full 30-year period under the "injury" provision in the policy. Western National agreed to that as the trial started.

The second count sought compensatory and punitive damages against the company and the claims supervisor for conspiring to sell Fletcher a policy they didn't intend to honor. Compensatory damages would have compensated Fletcher for the benefits he felt his policy should have provided him. Punitive damages would have punished the defendant for the alleged wrongdoing. The second count was dismissed by the judge.

The third also sought compensatory and punitive damages, and accused the firm and the claims supervisor of inflicting emotional distress on their customer. That complaint went to trial and was heard in Orange County by Superior Court Judge William S. Lee and a jury.

The attempt to save $50,400 ended up costing Western National $60,000 in compensatory damages and $180,000 in punitive damages. And, considering the jury's original decision to award Fletcher $710,000 in punitive damages, the firm got off rather easily.

The appellate court upheld the award in 1970, and the Supreme Court declined even to review the case when Western National appealed. Eventually, Fletcher was compensated, although to avoid any further delay he agreed to take an amount less than the jury award.

Justice Marcus Kaufman of the Fourth District Court of Appeal wrote the 1970 opinion in the case. Summarizing the trial, Kaufman wrote that a Western National executive "faced with the bleak prospect (of the firm being liable for 30 years of payments) . . . immediately set about to find some way of minimizing or avoiding plaintiff's claim."

If no contingency fee system had existed, however, Fletcher's options would have been very simple. Option one: Come up with a sizable retainer for his lawyer and commit to pay the balance of his lawyer's fee, win or lose, and possibly the legal expenses incurred by the insurance company if his case were lost. Option two: Don't go to court at all and accept the insurance company's action.

Fortunately, the contingency fee system did exist, and Fletcher was able to find an attorney who was willing to take the case on the condition that he would be paid only if he won. To get an idea of attorney Hews's investment in Fletcher's case, just consider this timetable. Fletcher's injury occurred in January 1965. In October 1966, he turned the threatening letters he had received from the insurance company over to Hews. In February 1967, after numerous exchanges of correspondence between lawyers, the lawsuit was filed. The trial began in February 1968, and when it concluded the insurance company immediately appealed Fletcher's victory. Finally, in October 1970—four years after Fletcher's attorney took the case—the California Supreme Court rejected the insurance company's appeal and cleared the way for Fletcher to collect payment of the punitive damages and for Hews to collect his fee. Up until that time, all the costs of the lawsuit and trial had been borne by Hews.

And that is the system the defense lobby wants to eliminate, or, at least, make so unattractive for experienced lawyers that the Mary Anne Rodriguezes, Louisa Muskopfs and U.L. Fletchers of the world won't be able to find an attorney with experience equal to that possessed by highly paid veteran defense lawyers.

The concept of the contingency, or result fee, is not peculiar to the law. An investor who puts up a "grubstake" for a prospector and makes money if the prospector finds gold or silver or whatever, engages in contingency investing. If the prospector comes up empty, the investor comes up empty. The same relationship exists between today's highly praised venture capitalists who provide start-up money for exciting new enterprises. If the enterprise is successful, the investors profit. If it is not, they don't.

Nor is the contingency fee concept new in law. Legal scholar Max Radin, a professor at the University of California School of Jurisprudence some 40 years ago, explored the contingency fee concept in an article he wrote for the *California Law Review*. "We have in an oration of Isaeus (in the 4th century B.C.) the statement that Melas prosecuted a claim of Diacaeogenes on the understanding that he was to receive half of the proceeds," Radin wrote.

Melas probably wasn't a lawyer, as we use the term today. Sometime around the 6th century B.C., Radin wrote, ". . . it was made possible for kindly men to come to the assistance of such wretches as poor and friendless plaintiffs" in matters before the courts of the time. It was also not uncommon, Radin said, for wealthy persons to purchase the claim of someone who had been wronged and prosecute it in his place, keeping whatever proceeds were awarded. The purchase of someone else's grievance was often done by persons harboring an unsatisfied grievance of their own against the defendant, and developed into a practice called "champerty," which was usually prohibited by nations that had written laws.

The Greeks and then the Romans permitted the practice of a claimant being represented in court by an advocate, but Roman law prohibited the advocate from collecting a fee. He could be given a gift by the plaintiff if the lawsuit was successful, but his compensation was more likely to be in the form of increased esteem among his peers and, perhaps, an opportunity for political advancement.

Despite the strong opposition of the wealthy to the practice of champerty and the concept of a client and his lawyer sharing the proceeds of a civil lawsuit, the arrangement seems to have persisted well into the Middle Ages. Since the most important suits were suits for the recovery of land, Radin wrote, the contingency fee for the successful plaintiff's lawyer was usually a portion of the recovered property. Since ownership of land was perhaps the most accepted measure of wealth at the time, the station of the successful lawyer in class-conscious England rose as his property holdings increased.

But then, as now, while there were lawyers whose prime focus was on improving their station by making as much money and acquiring as much property as they could, there were also lawyers who were outraged at injustices and worked hard to overcome them. Then, as now, there were lawyers who understood that the privilege of practicing their profession included a responsibility to see that fairness was done to individuals who were unable to protect themselves against assaults on fairness by the powerful.

The modern-day concept of the contingency fee began developing during the industrial revolution, when factory owners gave little or no heed to worker safety. Most workers mangled or burned in industrial accidents and unable to return to their jobs were simply let go by their companies. It doesn't require much imagination to appreciate the straits a suddenly disabled worker and his family would be in under such a circumstance. The disabled worker couldn't put food on his family's table, much less advance funds to retain a lawyer to fight the employer whose negligence had caused him to be injured, unemployed, and impoverished. Fortunately, there were some public-minded lawyers willing to represent injured workers without a guarantee of compensation, and they began taking employers into court. If they won their case—not, by any means, a certainty—they got paid. If they didn't win, they didn't get paid.

A unanimous United States Supreme Court in 1877 affirmed the legality of the contingency fee in a strange case that illustrates why clients and attorneys need written contracts. A lawyer named Robert J. Atkinson had been retained by a firm seeking compensation from the federal government for "certain steamers, which were used by the United States during the war of the rebellion."

Atkinson, working for a contingency fee, vigorously prosecuted the case over a five-year period, and the government finally settled before the trial and agreed to pay the $45,925.07 sought in the suit. Before the check was delivered, however, Atkinson died. The plaintiff firm then refused to pay his fee, saying not only that the lawyer didn't need it anymore, but that the contingency fee agreement it had made with him was itself illegal. Atkinson's heirs sued for the fee, won in a lower court, then were taken for a seven-year trip through the appellate process by the steamship firm.

In his opinion, U.S. Supreme Court Justice Nathan Clifford pointed out that in the preparing and prosecuting of lawsuits "there is frequently and necessarily required a degree of knowledge and skill, and an acquaintance with forms and principles, not possessed by the unlettered citizen, before a person can obtain that which is justly his due." It is ". . . the settled rule of law in this court (that a contingency fee agreement) is beyond legitimate controversy," and ". . . courts of justice (may not) adjudge (contingency fee) contracts illegal, if they are free of any taint of fraud, misrepresentation, or unfairness."

Clifford and his associate justices upheld the lower court jury's finding that Atkinson's estate should receive an appropriate percentage of the settlement, specifically $9,185.28, or a little more than 20 percent for his five years of work.

Despite the U.S. Supreme Court's unanimous assertion more than a century ago that the contingency fee's legality was a "settled rule of law," challenges have continued. The results of subsequent legal challenges have only confirmed the 1877 opinion, but the court's further assertion that the contingency fee was "beyond legitimate controversy" was obviously a flawed conclusion.

The most blatant frontal attack to date came in November 1988, in a California election campaign. The insurance industry placed three initiatives on the ballot—Propositions 101, 104, and 106—including in each of them provisions sharply limiting the contingency fees lawyers and their clients could agree to in written contracts. The contingency fee was the principal target of the industry's incredible $74 million California campaign expenditure, and industry spokespersons admitted candidly that the objective of the attack on the contingency fee was "less litigation."

Success would have restricted the ability of low- and moderate-income consumers and employees to contract for representation with an experienced personal injury lawyer if they believed they had been injured because of someone else's negligence. Fortunately, California's wise voters recognized the three initiatives for what they were and rejected them.

Consider the result had the insurance industry triumphed and the contingency fee system, for all practical purposes, been abolished. Just as many people would have suffered just as many injuries from just as much negligence in a world without contingency fees as they suffer now. The difference would be that juries wouldn't have the opportunity to determine responsibility.

In a just world, victims would be compensated for their injuries. In a logical world, wrongdoers would be punished if their wrongdoing caused injury. But in the world the defense lobby is seeking, victims would not be compensated and wrongdoers would not be punished, because the grievances would never make it into court. Committing or underwriting negligence would be risk-free.

The three insurance industry ballot proposals in California in 1988 would have limited a plaintiff's attorney's contingency fee in a case to far less than the income of defense attorneys working either on salary or for an hourly rate (who, by the way, are paid in full even if they lose the case).

The three ballot measures were rejected, but the concept did not disappear. A bill proposing restrictions on contingency fees was introduced in the California Legislature early in 1989, and similar legislation was sponsored in Congress. Contingency fee limits have already been established in Connecticut, Florida, and New Jersey, and proposals have been introduced in the legislatures of several other states. Many states, including California, have placed restrictions on the fees lawyers can obtain in medical malpractice lawsuits in an effort to bring skyrocketing medical malpractice insurance rates under control. Unfortunately, no study has been made yet of the effect of the restrictions on either the number of medical malpractice lawsuits filed or the cost of malpractice insurance.

Critics of the contingency fee concept contend that it "encourages litigation, invites litigants to press frivolous claims, increases the size of judgments, and forces out-of-court settlements of insurance claims," according to a May 1986 article in *Washington Watch*, distributed by the Business Action Network. That pretty well typifies the criticism, so let's take a close look at it.

First, it states, the availability of lawyers willing to work for a contingency fee ". . . encourages litigation." Well, what are the alternatives to litigation if the party causing the injury refuses to do the right thing and compensate the injured person? If, for instance, the government agencies assigned to designing a flood control system allow a levee to be built that they know—KNOW—ahead of time is inadequate to hold back the waters of a river at peak flow, should the tax-paying property owners who helped finance the design and construction of the levee just shrug their shoulders and say, "That's life, you win some and you lose some," when the river breaks through and destroys their homes and their crops and imposes a financial burden far in excess of any insurance they might have?

That's one alternative. Do nothing. Another is to organize a march and burn down City Hall, or the State House, or the regional office of the Army Corps of Engineers, or the factory producing a defective, injury-causing product. Violence has always been some people's response to an unsatisfied grievance. Given those two alternatives, is something that "encourages litigation"—if that litigation is meritorious—really something evil?

Next, the contingency fee "invites litigants to press frivolous claims." "Frivolous," according to my dictionary, means "of little weight, worth, or importance; not worthy of serious notice." Is there an incentive for lawyers to file frivolous lawsuits? Filing any lawsuit requires that papers be prepared and put across the desk at the courthouse. There has to be some preliminary investigations conducted, records examined, and witnesses interviewed, and that all requires some expenditure of time and money. And lawyers working for a contingency fee, remember, are not compensated for any work they do unless they win the case and their client receives some money.

A jury consisting of six or 12 of your neighbors is not going to find for a plaintiff whose claim is "not worthy of serious notice." As a matter of fact, a judge would probably not let a frivolous suit even get to a jury. So just exactly what is the incentive for a lawyer to file a lawsuit he knows is frivolous?

Critics have an answer for that one, they say. Lawsuits, even frivolous ones, are nuisances, and sometimes a defendant will settle a suit just to spare himself or herself the nuisance of fighting it. Which brings us to criticism three, that the contingency fee "forces the out-of-court settlement of insurance claims." Nothing is "forced" on anybody, of course. If a defendant chooses to settle a claim believed to be frivolous, without merit, just to save the aggravation of a trial, then that certainly invites the filing of frivolous claims. If the defendant chooses to settle a frivolous claim because the expense of a trial, even if the case is won, might exceed the settlement amount, that also encourages the filing of frivolous suits.

A defendant choosing to settle a suit sometimes does it because, bless the thought, it is simply the right thing for the injured plaintiff. It could also mean the defendant fears a jury might award an even bigger sum than is being offered as a settlement.

So, even though the defense lobby hasn't asked for my advice, I'll give it anyhow. Don't settle suits you believe to be frivolous. Fight them, tooth and nail. You'll do two things. You'll discourage such filings, because you'll win those lawsuits that are truly without merit and the plaintiff's lawyers won't be paid for their time and expense. And, you'll learn quickly enough to distinguish between lawsuits that are legitimate and those that aren't.

Same advice for plaintiffs' lawyers. If you file a frivolous suit and the defendants fight it and a judge or jury agrees, the defendants will win and you'll receive no compensation for any work you've done or expense you've incurred. Those of you who are unable to distinguish between legitimate and frivolous claims are going to become poor in a hurry. Those of you who are greedy (and dumb) enough to file frivolous suits in the hope of forcing harassed defendants to settle will lose your bets if the defendants fight back, and, hopefully, you'll turn to some other line of work.

And, by the way, what about the "frivolous defense" or "frivolous appeal" that defense lawyers use just to string out a lawsuit in hopes of wearing down the plaintiff? If a plaintiff of low or limited income who sues and wins is given a choice between taking a lesser sum than the jury awarded right now, or waiting a year or two or perhaps three until an appeal runs its course before collecting, what real choice is there?

The defense lawyer who deliberately uses a frivolous defense or files a frivolous appeal gets paid anyway, while a plaintiff's lawyer, to make the point one more time, gets paid only if the result is good for the client. If the result is not good, no fee is paid. The contingency fee, then, would seem to be a barrier against the filing of frivolous lawsuits, but the benefit members of the defense lobby receive from that is evidently outweighed, in their minds, by the access to the legal process the contingency fee system gives to people.

There is an irony in the defense lobby's attempt to limit contingency fees that shouldn't be overlooked. They are trying to restrict people's freedom to enter into a contract by controlling the price of the service people wish to purchase. The defense lobby—primarily big business—is promoting price controls! If you want to see a business owner turn red-faced angry in a hurry, mention the phrase "government price controls."

While the defense lobby doesn't want ordinary consumers to be able to hire attorneys on a contingent fee basis, those big corporate law firms that usually represent members of the defense lobby don't mind making good use of the system if there's a chance to make money doing it. "Pressed by spiraling costs and growing competition," said a March 21, 1989 *Wall Street Journal* story, "many old-line law firms now see contingency arrangements as a risk sometimes worth taking." But the risk can be substantial, the *Journal* added. "Major commercial litigation can drag on for years without the firm receiving any fee. If the firm loses, it forfeits its investment."

The *Journal* provided details of one risk that paid off big for a Houston law firm, Vinson & Elkins. The firm filed a federal antitrust lawsuit in 1984 for several corporate clients, and invested $15 million in the case before receiving its first return three years later when two of the defendants settled their cases. Before a jury finally returned a $1.04 billion damage verdict against Santa Fe Southern Pacific Co. a week before the *Journal* story, Vinson & Elkins had invested $25 million in the litigation. An appeal could require several years' more work by the law firm, and additional expense, but if the verdict is upheld, the firm could collect more than

$300 million in contingency fees.

If it had lost in the trial court, or if the appeal is successful, much of the firm's $25 million-plus investment would be lost. If the damage award is reduced substantially, the return on the investment, over the six- or seven- or eight-year period from filing of the lawsuit to collection, could be considerably less than spectacular. If the verdict stands, however, "I think, frankly, our success will pique the interest of a lot of law firms," a Vinson & Elkins spokesman said.

The primary purpose of the contingency fee system, however, is not to provide an alternative form of financing lawsuits for big business, but to provide access to the legal system to people who can't afford to guarantee payment for a lawyer's time. True, Mary Anne Rodriguez and U.L. Fletcher didn't need lawyers to gain access to the system. She could have filed suit against McDonnell-Douglas and Bethlehem Steel and the other two corporate defendants without a lawyer, and he could have taken the Western National Life Insurance Co. into court all by himself. The law allowed them to do that.

Would you have bothered to do that?

Having "access" to the legal system without a lawyer reminds me of a statement attributed to Anatole France, praising, tongue in cheek, "The majestic egalitarianism of the law, which forbids rich and poor alike to sleep under bridges, to beg in the streets, and to steal bread."

For Mary Anne Rodriguez, Louisa Muskopf, U.L. Fletcher, and the other victims mentioned in this book, and the hundreds of thousands of others not mentioned, the contingency fee system provided an opportunity to seek justice. And "justice," in their cases, was not some abstract concept. "Justice" meant food on the table, some measure of independence for Mary Anne, some chance at opportunity for U.L. Fletcher's children.

Justice for future victims is in peril, because the forces trying to shut and lock the courthouse door are formidable and very, very determined. It is, after all, the amount of their profits that are at risk. To insulate those profits from risk, they are willing to make an investment of astonishing magnitude. I left out a word. To insulate those profits from risk, they are willing to make a *contingency* investment of astonishing magnitude.

Think how much they will win, if they win.

6

A Simple Business Decision

Quite possibly no single case more graphically illustrates what could be lost if the defense lobby wins its long battle to close the courthouse doors to the less-than-wealthy than the famous Ford Pinto lawsuit. It is the best possible argument why the civil justice system we now have must be preserved, why the contingency fee system we now have must be preserved, why a jury's authority to impose punitive damages must be preserved.

Often in this book, in discussing the development and current use of what we call the "tort system," I have used the word "negligence" to describe how injuries come to be inflicted on innocent people. And because in the absence of negligence the injuries would not have occurred, why the victim should be compensated by the negligent party. But "negligence" doesn't begin to cover the circumstances in the Ford Pinto case.

A woman died and a young boy will suffer physical and

79

emotional scars the rest of his life from the horrifying seconds he spent trapped in a burning Pinto, because the Ford Motor Company weighed dollars and human lives, and made the simple business decision that dollars were more important.

Here is one response to the evidence produced at the six-month trial in 1977-78: "The conduct of Ford's management was reprehensible in the extreme. It exhibited a conscious and callous disregard of public safety in order to maximize corporate profits." That is not a lawyer for the dead woman's family or the burned boy talking. That is the formal written opinion from the three-judge Court of Appeal that denied Ford's request to overturn the results of the jury trial.

How about a description of the Pinto as "a lousy, unsafe product." That's still not a plaintiff's lawyer talking. That's the foreman of the jury, Andrew Quinn, talking to a *Wall Street Journal* reporter after the jury socked Ford with a $125 million punitive damage verdict. "We came up with this high amount so Ford wouldn't design cars this way again," Quinn told *Journal* reporter Roy J. Harris Jr.

Let me tell you why "negligence" is not an appropriate word to describe Ford's actions. Let me explain what the Court of Appeal meant by "a conscious and callous disregard of public safety."

May 28, 1972. Mrs. Lily Gray has to drive from her home in Anaheim, near Disneyland in Southern California, to the desert community of Barstow, 90 miles east, to take care of a family chore. She invites a neighbor, 13-year-old Richard Grimshaw, to accompany her and sets out in the Gray family's spanking new Pinto hatchback, purchased just six months earlier. While they are on Interstate 15, the Pinto suddenly stalls, and is hit in the rear by a 1962 Ford Galaxie.

What happens next is worse than terrible. It is worse than terrible because it need not have happened at all. Eleven dollars could have prevented it. Stephen K. Tamura, presiding justice of the appellate court that ruled on the case nine years later, provided some history about the 1972 Pinto Mrs. Gray was driving.

"In 1968," Justice Tamura's summary of the trial evidence states, "Ford began designing a new subcompact automobile which ultimately became the Pinto. Mr. (Lee) Iacocca, then a Ford vice president, conceived the project and was its moving force. Ford's objective was to build a car at or below 2,000 pounds to sell for no more than $2,000.

"Ordinarily marketing surveys and preliminary engineering studies precede the styling of a new automobile line. Pinto, however, was a rush project, so that styling preceded engineering and dictated engineering design to a greater degree than usual. Among the engineering decisions dictated by styling was the placement of the fuel tank. It was then the preferred practice in Europe and Japan to locate the gas tank over the rear axle in subcompacts because a small vehicle had less 'crush space' between the rear axle and the bumper than larger cars. The Pinto's styling, however, required the tank to be placed behind the rear axle, leaving only nine or 10 inches of 'crush space'—far less than in any other American automobile or Ford overseas compact. In addition, the Pinto was designed so that its bumper was little more than a chrome strip, less substantial than the bumper of any other American car produced then or later. The Pinto's rear structure also lacked reinforcing members known as 'hat sections' (two longitudinal side members) and horizontal cross-members running between them such as were found in cars of larger unitized construction and in all automobiles produced by Ford's overseas operations. The absence of the reinforcing members rendered the Pinto less crush resistant than other vehicles. Finally, the differential housing selected for the Pinto had an exposed flange and a line of exposed bolt heads. These protrusions were sufficient to puncture a gas tank driven forward against the differential upon rear impact."

The opinion then summarized, again from evidence given at the trial, details of crash tests conducted by Ford engineers on the Pinto. Harris described the tests in a *Wall Street Journal* story that appeared February 14, 1978, a week after the trial ended. The jury, the reporter wrote, saw the results of five tests of the Pinto fuel tank's crashworthiness. "(T)he tanks on experimentally crashed Pintos showed significant damage and leakage in each case," he wrote. In one test, the Pinto was "backed into a wall at 20 miles per hour and its tank, filled with a non-flammable substance, ruptured with such force it looked, (one juror said) 'like a fireman had stuck a hose inside the car and turned it on.'"

From the Appellate Court opinion:"Tests conducted by Ford on other vehicles, including modified or reinforced mechanical Pinto prototypes, proved safe at speeds at which the Pinto failed." Again, details of the tests are provided. Normally, Justice Tamura wrote, "When a prototype failed the fuel system integrity test, the standard of care for engineers in the (automobile) industry was to redesign and retest it. The vulnerability of the production Pinto's fuel tank at speeds of 20 and 30 miles per hour fixed barrier tests could have been remedied by inexpensive 'fixes,' but Ford produced and sold the Pinto to the public without doing anything to remedy the defects."

An internal Ford memorandum introduced into evidence at the trial placed the average cost of eliminating the problem at $11. The court opinion informs us that "Harley Copp, a former Ford engineer and executive in charge of the crash testing program, testified that the highest level of Ford's management made the decision to go forward with the production of the Pinto, knowing that the gas tank was vulnerable to puncture and rupture at low rear impact speeds, creating a significant risk of death or injury from fire, and knowing that 'fixes' were feasible at nominal cost. He testified that management's decision was based on the cost savings which would inure from omitting or delaying the 'fixes.'"

The internal Ford memo stated, with frightening clarity: "Implementation (of safety improvement) costs far (outweigh) the expected benefits." The word "benefits," obviously, applied to Ford's profit margin, not to the people who purchased and drove Pintos, or their passengers.

It certainly didn't apply to Lily Gray or Richard Grimshaw on that May day in 1972 when the Ford Galaxie plowed into the rear of the Pinto. In scant, horrifying seconds, the Pinto's fuel tank is driven forward, as tests indicated it would be. It is punctured, as tests indicated it would be. Gasoline is sent spurting into the interior of the car, as tests indicated it would be. The gasoline explodes into flames. Mrs. Gray, trapped inside the inferno, burns to death. Young Richard Grimshaw somehow extricates himself from the blazing wreckage, but he suffers burns over 90 percent of his body. His nose, his left ear, and much of his left hand, are destroyed. By the time of the trial, more than five years later, he has had 60 operations. He would have more.

Does the phrase "conscious and callous disregard for public safety" seem appropriate?

Following an exhausting six-month trial, the jury delivered its verdicts on Feb. 6, 1978—after, by the way, a mere 90 minutes of deliberation—awarding Mrs. Gray's family $560,000 and giving Richard Grimshaw $2 million in compensatory damages plus $125 million in punitive damages. Grimshaw's attorneys, Arthur N. Hews Jr. and Mark P. Robinson Jr. of Santa Ana, had asked the jury to assess Ford $100 million in punitive damages. The $100 million, they said, was about what Ford planned to save by not making the gas tank improvements in the Pinto's design. As jury foreman Quinn later explained to the *Wall Street Journal,* for Ford to be assessed only what it expected to save would be, in essence, a wash—no real loss at all. There should be a real penalty, he said the jury felt, so another $25 million was tacked on, making the $125 million total the largest punitive damage award ever given until then in a personal injury suit.

Actually, Robinson's estimate of the amount of money Ford expected to save was off the mark. According to the internal company memo he had obtained, accident statistics indicated that 180 burn deaths and another 100 serious burn injuries were likely in a given year, at an average cost to the company of $200,000 per death and $67,000 per injury. Those costs, plus the cost of compensating for burn damage to vehicles, would total $49.5 million. The cost of making safety improvements at $11 for each of 11 million cars and $11 for each of 1.5 million light trucks would total $137 million, the memo stated.

Let me pull all those numbers together. Ford estimated, and appears to have accepted the likelihood, that 180 people would be burned to death and 100 people would be injured if it did not fix the Pinto fuel tank problem officials *knew* existed. Since, according to the memo, "Implementation of safety improvements ($137 million) far outweighs the expected benefits (the $49.5 million Ford might save from lawsuits that wouldn't be filed because people wouldn't have been killed or injured or cars damaged)," Ford's decision not to fix the problem allowed it to keep an additional $87.5 million in its bank account.

Richard Grimshaw's punitive damage award, equal to about one month's profits for Ford, according to the *Journal* story, was so huge it startled Orange County Superior Court Judge Leonard Goldstein, and he reduced it to $3.5 million. "The judge explained later that he felt sure that Ford would appeal the jury's $125 million award and that Grimshaw wouldn't see any money at all for years," Robinson recalled. "He said he thought $3.5 million was an amount Ford would pay immediately. He was wrong, and he later expressed regret that he had been wrong."

Judge Goldstein said he could not recall the conversation cited by Robinson. He reduced the jury award, he said in a 1989 interview, because of its enormity. "You have to remember that this was in 1977, just prior to the inflationary spiral that made $20,000 homes suddenly worth $100,000 or more," the judge said. "If a similar case were before me now, I would undoubtedly come up with a different number at the end because the value of the dollar is different.

"The highest punitive damage award that had ever been made in California until then was, I think, $600,000, so I felt comfortable then and I'm comfortable now with imposing damages of more than five times the previous high. If ever a plaintiff deserved a substantial award, it was Richard Grimshaw, but there just was no criteria then for an award of this size, and I think the award I allowed provided adequate punishment and served, I believe, the deterrent effect that was appropriate. The appellate court agreed."

Both Ford and Grimshaw appealed. Both lost, and the $3.5 million award was allowed to stand. The official summary of the appellate court's decision stated there had been "ample evidence to support a finding of malice and corporate responsibility," that Ford knew of the danger and "could have corrected the design defects at minimal cost but deferred corrections by engaging in a cost-benefit analysis balancing human lives and limbs against corporate profits." The lowered $3.5 million award, the court held, "was well within reason considering the degree of reprehensibility of defendant's conduct, defendant's wealth, the amount of compensatory damages, and an amount that would serve as a deterrent to similar conduct."

The $3.5 million punitive damage award, in the court's view, served two purposes. It was punishment for "the reprehensibility of defendant's conduct" and it was "a deterrent to similar conduct."

Mrs. Gray's life ended and Richard Grimshaw's was forever altered on May 28, 1972. Their families became clients of attorneys Byron Rabin (for the Gray family), and Hews and Robinson late in 1973; and in January of 1974 Robinson began devoting the major part of his time to the case. The verdict was returned four years later, Feb. 6, 1978. After the appellate court upheld Judge Goldstein's ruling, Ford continued its appeal. The State Supreme Court declined to overturn the lower court rulings, and finally, late in 1981, the Gray and Grimshaw families received the money to which the civil justice system said they were entitled. And some nine years after taking the case, with, by his own estimate, hundreds of thousands of dollars of his firm's time and money expended for the lawsuit, Mark Robinson and his colleagues finally collected a fee.

Robinson was asked if he would have taken on the case had the contingency fee limits similar to those proposed in California by the insurance industry in 1988 and 1989 been in effect in the 1970s. "Had contingency fee limits such as those now being proposed been in effect in the '70s, the Grimshaw case just wouldn't have happened," he said. "And I'll tell you something else. If the Grimshaw case hadn't happened, if there hadn't been that huge jury award to get the attention of Ford and of the Department of Transportation in Washington, the Pinto wouldn't have been recalled and who knows how many other deaths and injuries from exploding fuel tanks there might have been. And that's not just speculation. People in Washington have told me it was our verdict that set things in motion and resulted in the recall."

The argument for the contingency fee concept seems overwhelming, but the defense lobby is nevertheless working hard to terminate it, just as it is trying to "save" society from the ravages of punitive damages. Richard J. Mahoney, chairman and chief executive officer of the Monsanto Company, articulated the defense lobby's antipathy for punitive damages in an article for the *New*

York Times in 1988. Punitive damages, he wrote, are "an anomaly peculiar to the United States and are virtually unknown in the world's remaining civil-law countries." The idea, of course, is to portray punitive damages as some sort of recent Yankee aberration that really sophisticated nations disdain.

The concept, however, is hardly new, and is certainly not confined to the United States. Among the judgments Moses brought down from the mountain, according to Chapter 22 of Exodus, was this: "If a man shall steal an ox, or a sheep, and kill it, or sell it; he shall restore five oxen for an ox, and four sheep for a sheep." True, Moses was speaking about punishment for theft, and personal injury lawsuits are tried in civil rather than criminal courts. But the judgment does show that the concept of combining compensation and punishment existed in Biblical times, and went beyond merely restoring to a victim only what he or she had lost.

In the Roman law of the fourth century, Emperor Constantine Augustus decreed that the area immediately surrounding state storehouses was to be kept vacant because of the danger of fire. "But," he ordered, "if any person through love of building should disregard public damage, We direct that not only what he constructed, but all his property and whatever he had in his own right, shall be (confiscated)." Confiscation of all property is a harsh penalty for violating what we today would call a zoning ordinance, a part of the civil law, but I imagine the decree's real and intended value was in deterring anyone whose "love of building" might tempt him to ignore the ordinance.

In our civil law, the phrase "exemplary damages" is used interchangeably with "punitive damages," and nothing better illustrates the dual function of the concept than the two legal phrases that describe it. "Punitive," of course, refers to "punishment." "Exemplary" means, in part, "serving as a warning."

Thomas F. Lambert Jr., for 33 years the editor-in-chief of

publications distributed by the Association of Trial Lawyers of America, has written extensively on punitive damages. In one article, titled "Commercial Litigation," he cites a 1763 case in England in which a judge, Lord Camden, first used the terms "exemplary" and "punitive" damages. Lord Camden, Lambert wrote, "expressed judicial outrage at defendants' highhandedness in unlawfully invading plaintiff's house under a general warrant and (held) that defendants could properly be (assessed) punitive damages." The defendant public officials were seen by the jury to have been "exercising arbitrary power, violating Magna Charta, and attempting to destroy the liberty of the Kingdom" by their unlawful invasion of the plaintiff's home. Lambert added, "These are the ideas which struck the jury on the trial, and I think they have done right in giving exemplary damages."

In a later English case, an appellate judge upheld a 500 pound award in a land trespass case, writing "(I)n a case where a man disregards every principle which actuates the conduct of gentlemen, what is to restrain him except large damages?"

Another legal scholar, University of Iowa Law Professor Dorsey D. Ellis Jr., wrote in a November 1982 edition of the *University of Southern California Law Review* devoted to punitive damages: "The common law authority for courts to award punitive damages originated in 18th century England, in cases in which defendants challenged and sought to have set aside large, arguably excessive jury verdicts."

Professor Ellis cites an appellate ruling in England in which a punitive damage award was upheld. The court stated a jury had authority "to give damages for more than the injury received. Damages are designed not only as satisfaction for the injured person, but likewise as punishment to the guilty, to deter from any such proceeding for the future, and as proof of the detestation of the jury to the action itself."

There are really seven purposes for punitive damages, Professor Ellis wrote. In addition to (1) punishment; and (2) deterring similar conduct in the future by the defendant; punitive or exemplary damages also (3) deter others from similar misconduct; (4) preserve the peace (so, as one appellate court stated, according to Lambert, a victim could exact "private revenge ... carried out in the courts rather than through duels or in back alleys"); (5) induce private law enforcement (to help protect society against civil wrongdoing); (6) compensate plaintiffs for losses that are otherwise not compensable; and (7) enable the plaintiff's attorney to be compensated.

A 1983 opinion by the federal district court in Oklahoma supports Ellis's contention that punitive damages preserve social peace. The opinion, Lambert wrote in a comprehensive 1988 monograph, *The Case for Punitive Damages*, holds that "punitive damages are designed to benefit society rather than the individual plaintiff-victim. The plaintiff acts as a private attorney general to punish and deter future social misconduct, thereby encouraging adherence to safety standards that benefit consumers generally."

To have the desired deterrent effect, the court (in *Thiry v. Armstrong World Industries*) said, "The penalty must directly attack the profit incentive generated by the marketing misconduct. The award should not only take away any profit realized from the single sale to the plaintiff, but also the profits realized from other such sales of the defective product to others . . . . The penalty should not only match the misconduct but of necessity should relate to the wealth of the wrongdoer."

That, of course, was the logic used by the jury in the Grimshaw case against the Ford Motor Company. It imposed punitive damages it thought related to the wealth of the company. The trial court judge reduced the award, but in upholding the reduced $3.5 million punitive damage award, the appellate court made a

89

telling observation that explains why victims must have a recourse other than government regulation to protect them against negligence by the manufacturers and sellers of goods and services. "It is precisely because monetary penalties under government regulations prescribing business standards or the criminal law are so inadequate and inefficient as deterrents against a manufacturer and distributor of mass-produced products," the court wrote, "that punitive damages must be of sufficient amount to discourage such practices," as the Ford Motor Company's in the Pinto case. The court apparently was correct, because Ford hastily redesigned the Pinto's gas tank.

Lambert writes,"Most American courts will allow juries to award punitive damages to discourage repetition of defendant's misconduct and to make an example of him in two kinds of cases: (1) against defendants guilty of intentional misconduct of an outrageous or oppressive nature; and, (2) against those guilty of reckless and wanton disregard of safety or rights."

Because most providers of goods and services are aware they have a "duty of due care" and do not place consumers in jeopardy, the circumstances that persuade juries to impose punitive damages rarely occur. But even so, although it is only outrageous misconduct that is punished, the defense lobby argues that all of its members should be free from such risk. It has persuaded the legislatures of two states, Louisiana and Nebraska, to prohibit imposition of punitive damages under any circumstances. Three other states, Massachusetts, Washington, and Indiana, limit punitive damage awards to specific kinds of cases. In addition, a number of other states in recent years have placed various kinds of limits on jury discretion by enacting defense lobby-sponsored "tort reform" legislation.

A counter offensive succeeded in Washington in 1989 when that state's Supreme Court, responding to an appeal by a pipefitter harmed by exposure to asbestos, declared a provision of recently enacted tort reform law limiting punitive damage awards in personal injury suits unconstitutionally "interferes with the jury's traditional function to determine damages." Florida's Supreme Court has also struck down a legislatively imposed cap on non-economic losses, stating: "A plaintiff who receives a jury verdict for ... $1 million has not received a constitutional redress of injuries if the legislature statutorily and arbitrarily caps the recovery at $450,000." Similar conclusions have been reached by the supreme courts of Kansas, Texas, and Wyoming.

George McMonagle, an Ohio jurist, wrote in 1985: "Simply stated, the legislative scheme of shifting responsibility for loss from one of the most affluent segments of society to those who are most unable to sustain the burden, i.e., horribly injured or maimed individuals, is not only inconceivable, but shocking to this court's conscience."

UCLA law professor Gary T. Schwartz, writing for the same *USC Law Review* issue cited earlier, presented the argument for punitive damages in starkly simple terms that any business executive can understand. "If punitive damages do indeed deter," Schwartz wrote, "it is due to the economic principle that adding to the cost of an activity necessarily decreases its frequency."

The civil justice system's provision for punitive damages allowed the Ford Pinto jury to reflect the passionate outrage of the community by imposing a substantial penalty. The system allowed the judge to reduce a penalty he thought excessive. The system would have allowed an appellate court to reduce the penalty still further, or eliminate it altogether if it thought that action was appropriate. But, despite those safeguards, the defense lobby wants the system changed because it *does* allow juries to determine originally an appropriate penalty, and that places business in a risk situation it can't control or predict.

Punitive damages, particularly the million dollar-plus awards that attract press attention, are awarded relatively rarely, and the amount actually collected by a successful plaintiff is often far less than the amount awarded by a jury. Nevertheless, punitive damages serve a purpose. They make careless or wrongful conduct costly, when someone is injured as a consequence. The Mississippi Supreme Court perhaps summed up the arguments for punitive damages most succinctly in 1985 when, in upholding a substantial cash punishment against an insurance company, it said, "In this kind of case it is the medicine most likely to cure the malady."

7

SAFETY IN THE MARKETPLACE

Pretend for a moment that you are someone who loves working with wood in your garage workshop. You are really pleased with the combination power tool you received for Christmas. You've been making some fancy legs for a table on the machine's lathe, and they've been turning out just as you'd hoped they would. You're working on the lathe one day in your workshop, with a large piece of wood locked securely into place. Suddenly, the wood flies out of the machine and strikes you squarely on the forehead, inflicting painful injuries.

You begin to suffer severe headaches that won't go away. A complaint to the store where the lathe was purchased provides no satisfaction, and a letter to the lathe's manufacturer doesn't even rate a reply. You're looking at protracted medical treatment for your continuing headaches, you're afraid to use the lathe anymore because you can't see anything wrong with it. You don't know what to do.

A neighbor knows a lawyer. Wouldn't hurt to talk to a lawyer, the neighbor says. I don't think a lawyer charges anything just to talk if it's an injury case, the neighbor says. So, somewhat reluctantly, you talk to a lawyer. You tell the lawyer what happened, tell him you followed the user's manual precisely, tell him you have a headache and it hurts.

The lawyer says you might have a case. He knows some power tool experts, engineers, who should look at the lathe. They run some tests, and discover that the set screws designed to hold the locking mechanism in place work loose because of the machine's normal vibration when it is being used. There are other, more efficient ways to hold the locking mechanism in place, ways that other lathe manufacturers use, the engineers say. Clearly a design defect, they tell the lawyer and the lawyer tells you. You've got a case. If the manufacturer doesn't agree to compensate you, sue, he says. It doesn't, and you do.

Essentially, that's the story of William B. Greenman, who was given a Shopsmith, a combination lathe-drill-saw, by his wife in 1955; was injured by it two years later; sued; won a jury verdict for $65,000; and, finally, in January of 1963, collected his money when the California Supreme Court unanimously rejected the manufacturer's appeal and upheld the jury verdict.

But this is another one of those cases whose significance goes far beyond its immediate import. It established in law two related principles that have ever since worked to make life a little safer for all of us. The court held that a "manufacturer is strictly liable in tort when an article he places on the market, knowing that it is to be used without inspection for defects, proves to have a defect that causes injury to a human being."

It also held that to establish the liability of the manufacturer, it was sufficient that the buyer "prove that he was injured while using the tool in a way it was intended to be used as a result of a defect in design and manufacture of which he was not aware that made the tool unsafe for its intended use."

Substitute the word "product" for the word "tool," and you can appreciate the significance of the *Greenman* case. You also become acquainted with a two-word phrase that gives manufacturers heartburn: product liability.

In an important way, the *Greenman* case was the beginning of the current war on consumer rights, because it established the consumer's right to safe products. *Greenman* brought accountability to product manufacturers; they fought it fiercely then, and they fight it fiercely now.

Product liability is a field of law based on a notion that some manufacturers evidently feel is outlandish, unfair, and unworkable. The notion, simply stated: Consumers have a right to assume that a purchased product will not harm them if it is used as intended. Or, as the California Supreme Court put it in a subsequent decision (*Barker v. Lull Engineering Co., Inc.*), a purchased product should "perform as safely as an ordinary consumer would expect when used in an intended or reasonably foreseeable manner."

The principle that a consumer should be able to use a product as it was intended to be used without being harmed by it was first applied to unwholesome food products, Justice Roger Traynor wrote in the landmark product liability case, *Greenman v. Yuba Power Products, Inc.* The *Greenman* case expanded what we now call "product liability" beyond food products. It's really not such a far-fetched notion that there's no real difference, as far as responsibility goes, between a person being harmed by consuming tainted food purchased from a grocery store and a person harmed by using a purchased product that turns out to be unsafe. In each case, the consumer has purchased and used something that would not have been on the market in the first place had reasonable care been exercised.

The early history of product safety in the United States is full of real horror stories. In those days, much to the satisfaction of manufacturers, contract law and not tort law ruled the world of commerce, and all anyone needed to know was summed up in the phrase "caveat emptor"—let the buyer beware. All too often the phrase should have been taken literally. In one of the more infamous examples of early product law, the Massengil Company marketed a liquid miracle drug that killed nearly 100 people within weeks of its introduction to the market. The president of the company later stated, "My chemists and I deeply regret the fatal results, but there was no error in the manufacturing of the product. We have been supplying legitimate professional demand, and not once could have foreseen the unlooked for results. I do not feel that there was any responsibility on our part."

Early court decisions were blunt not only in denying any rights to an injured consumer but about their reasons for doing so. In a famous English case in 1842 (*Winterbottom v. Wright*) a passenger in a mail coach was seriously injured when the coach collapsed for lack of proper maintenance. The company contracted to keep the coach in repair was clearly liable and the court was quite willing to grant a verdict to the owner of the coach for the cost of the repairs. But when it came time to consider the plight of the poor injured passenger, the court was appalled at even the suggestion that he should be compensated for his injuries. Lord Abinger predicted that to consider such a thing would lead to "the most absurd and outrageous consequences, to which I can see no limit unless we confine the operation of such contracts as this to the parties who entered into them."

In the face of increasing hazards in the marketplace, the government of the United States began a halting movement to impose some safety regulations. Such agencies as the Food and Drug Administration, the Occupational Safety and Health Administration, and the Consumer Product Safety Administration were created to develop and enforce guidelines. But while these regulations speak to the responsibilities of the producer or manufacturer, they ignore the subject of what compensation is appropriate for someone who has been harmed because those regulations were violated. The regulations usually provide for punishment for violators, but in too many cases the enforcement is impractical and ineffective and the punishment is insufficient to really motivate a manufacturer or producer to place a significantly greater emphasis on consumer safety.

All too often, a business person is presented with a simple business decision: Which will cost me more money, improving the safety of the product, or paying the government fine I'll be hit with if the product harms someone and if I'm caught? If the decision is to take the risk—or, really, to allow consumers to take the risk—there's little or nothing government can do beyond imposing the fine the risk-taker is willing to pay.

Fortunately, there is a process capable of making the risk unacceptable to manufacturers, of providing the incentive—the only incentive some business persons understand—to give greater consideration to product safety. That incentive is the risk of punitive damages imposed by a jury hearing a personal injury lawsuit.

Ralph Nader, in a 1989 letter to The Brookings Institution in Washington, DC, cited some examples of how the incentive provided by personal injury lawsuit awards has worked. Nader wrote, "We know that the Dalkon Shield IUD was removed from the U.S. market and recalled worldwide as a result of U.S. liability litigation. Other major products, too numerous to list, include: The Ford Pinto's exploding gas tank, redesigned after litigation; baby clothes made from 'Flannelette,' only slightly less flammable than newspaper, removed from the market after litigation; Drano's exploding container, redesigned after litigation; firefighter respirators which failed in a fire and killed three firefighters, redesigned after litigation. Strong product liability laws are the means of protection for tens of millions of Americans who are less likely to be injured because of the impact of lawsuits brought by prior victims."

The idea that a consumer has a right to assume he or she will not be harmed if a purchased product is used properly seems like such a basic truth that a challenge to it seems unreasonable on its face. But challenges there have been and challenges there will be. From manufacturers, of course.

The challenges take two forms. One seeks immunity from product liability laws and regulations, claiming the threat of law-suits and the potential of punitive damages discourages manufacturers from marketing products. Pharmaceutical firms, for instance, say they are reluctant to put medications on the market, even if they have been approved by the Food and Drug Administration, because one person in 10,000 might have an unpredictable reaction, sue, and win in court.

That does happen. Rarely. A study for the American Bar Association found punitive damages were awarded in only 3.8 percent of the verdicts in New York City, Chicago's Cook County, and Los Angeles County. Juries award punitive damages only when defendants have been proven to have behaved maliciously, or to have displayed a conscious disregard for the well-being of the public, or to have committed deliberate fraud. Punitive damages are not imposed without reason; and if, for some reason, a jury did let its indignation get in the way of good judgment, the trial judge or an appellate court can set aside or reduce the award, as occurred in Richard Grimshaw's suit against the Ford Motor Company.

Johnson and Johnson has also benefitted from that fact that courts, not juries, have the last word in the civil justice system. According to a company executive who testified in 1989 before a California legislative committee, Johnson and Johnson has been hit only three times in its history with punitive damage awards, and has never actually paid a dime.

So the argument that huge and unreasonable punitive damages have become so routine that the business enterprises don't dare market new products just doesn't hold up. Neither a jury nor a judge is going to punish a business firm that has exercised reasonable competence in the design and testing of a product before it is marketed.

Challenge two is the old refrain of "litigation explosion," this time tailored to product liability, with the claim that it is costing manufacturers huge sums of money for legal defense, to say nothing of the awards they have to pay when they lose. Again, the statistics just don't support that contention. Study after study, including the one I cited in Chapter 3 by the United States General Accounting Office, refutes the contention that a "litigation explosion" is paralyzing the country's court system.

The most interesting and most revealing studies have been done by the manufacturers themselves. For example, top corporate executives had worked themselves up into a lather of hostility toward product liability law by 1986. The Conference Board, a major research arm of big business, dutifully initiated a study of 232 major U.S. corporations with a minimum annual sales revenue of $100 million. The study, titled "Product Liability: The Corporate Response," polled the risk managers of the selected corporations, since obviously they would know better than anyone what the effects of product liability law were on their companies.

The results were fascinating and deserve to be quoted: "The most striking finding is that the impact of the liability issue seems far more related to rhetoric than to reality. Given all the media coverage and heated accusations, the so-called twin crises in product liability and insurance availability have left a relatively minor dent on the economics and organization of individual large firms, or on big business as a whole. In the words of one manager: 'There may be less here than meets the eye.'"

The report, as one can imagine, was not met with great enthusiasm by corporate leaders, who were actively trying to bang the drum and whip up public hysteria over product liability lawsuits. Particularly infuriating to the corporate heads was when "their" research group concluded that "Where product liability has had a notable impact—where it has most significantly affected management decision making—has been in the quality of the products themselves. Managers say products have become safer, manufacturing procedures have been improved, and labels and use instructions have become more explicit."

In other words, product liability law not only is not harming industry, but it works exactly the way it is intended to work. The threat of lawsuits makes manufacturers develop safer products. One can imagine the corporate fury brought down upon the heads of the poor researchers at the Conference Board when its study was released. The researchers were sent back to their research. A second study, released in 1988 and titled "The Impact of Product Liability," surveyed 500 chief executive officers (CEOs) about their views on the impact of product liability, and, predictably, articulated the desired theme: "The rapid growth in product liability litigation, as well as the hazards associated with substantial jury awards, has had a significant impact on corporate America."

There was a little problem about how to finesse the earlier report that had so clearly devastated their propaganda position. No problem; just a little note from the president of the Conference Board that refers to the earlier report and says: "Many of these managers reported that their companies, while experiencing cost increases, were 'adapting' to their problems with product liability, including the proliferation of lawsuits and the rise in insurance costs."

Now of course that is not at all what the earlier report had said, but it is a brilliant example of corporate public relations at its finest. To borrow a phrase from the first Conference Board report's conclusion, the language in the second report was obviously "far more related to rhetoric than to reality." In the battle to absolve the CEOs and their companies from responsibility for the injuries they cause, truth has been one of the first casualties.

The statistics don't dissuade the critics of product liability from continuing their efforts to prevent persons injured by their products from getting into court, however. It's an unusual state legislature that hasn't considered a proposal to immunize manufacturers and producers from liability when a consumer is injured. And sadly, in some states some measure of success has been achieved.

If product liability laws and regulations are eliminated or diminished to benefit manufacturers, the monetary incentive for manufacturers to give greater emphasis to consumer safety similarly will be eliminated or diminished. And that, of course, increases the risk to consumers. Product liability law is our best defense against hazardous goods. The Rand Corporation in Santa Monica looked at the issue in 1983. Its report, *Designing Safer Products: Corporate Response to Product Liability Laws and Regulations,* concluded simply that ". . . of all the various external social pressures influencing product design decisions, product liability seems to be the most influential."

8

A MATTER OF FAIRNESS

The year-old 1967 Oldsmobile was driven northbound on Alvarado Street in Los Angeles. About 70 feet from the intersection, the driver, Nga Li, seeing a sizable gap in southbound traffic, turned left, intending to enter a service station. She didn't make it. A taxicab accelerated through a yellow light southbound on Alvarado, and hit the Oldsmobile broadside, hard. The Oldsmobile was damaged, and so was Nga Li.

She sued, and set in motion one of the most important changes in California's civil justice history.

The trial court threw Nga Li's lawsuit out, accepting the defense argument that the plaintiff had contributed to the accident by misjudging the speed of the taxicab. The driver of the taxi was very negligent, and Nga Li's negligence, by comparison, was minor. No matter. Under the legal doctrine of contributory negligence then in effect, she was entitled to nothing. If a victim contributed to an automobile accident, the victim was not entitled to compensation. It didn't matter if the victim were only ten percent negligent, the careless driver who was 90 percent at fault escaped any and all legal and financial responsibility, and the poor victim went without compensation. That was the law.

This law, the doctrine of contributory negligence, was one of the most powerful tools members of the defense lobby had for avoiding responsibility for injuries they caused. At the time Nga Li sued, the only way injured victims could even hope to be compensated for the consequences of injuries caused by others was if they were virtually innocent, without a hint of blame. As in Nga Li's case, misjudging the excessive speed of an automobile about to shatter your life would create enough opening for the defendant to scream "contributory negligence" and get off scot-free, while the injured victim was forced to bear the full burden of the injuries primarily caused by someone else. In April 1975, the law changed. California Supreme Court Justice Raymond L. Sullivan, speaking for the majority in *Li v. Yellow Cab Company of California,* wrote, "The all-or-nothing rule of contributory negligence can be and ought to be superseded by a rule which assesses liability in proportion to fault.

"The doctrine of comparative negligence," Sullivan wrote, "is preferable to the . . . doctrine of contributory negligence from the point of view of logic, practical experience, and fundamental justice."

And so the rule in California now is comparative negligence; that is, liability in proportion to responsibility, or fault. If a jury determines one person is 90 percent responsible for an accident and the injured party is ten percent responsible, the person 90 percent responsible must pay 90 percent of the victim's medical and other costs resulting from the accident. The victim must absorb ten percent of the cost.

The law does change, but often it changes very, very slowly. That is appropriate because principles, once established in law, should be difficult to dislodge. You can imagine the chaos that would result if it were any other way. It's difficult enough to live by the rules without the rules changing constantly. Sometimes, though, it seems that changes come *too* slowly. When we look, now, at the two negligence concepts, we wonder how in the world the contributory negligence concept ever was accepted as law in the first place when the comparative negligence concept seems so much more fair. And why in the world did it take so long for so many states to get rid of a concept that so obviously, to quote Justice Sullivan, violated "fundamental justice?"

Legal scholars seem to agree that the concept of contributory negligence found its place in the law for practical economic reasons rather than as a consequence of the process of legal evolution. William Schwartz, in a 1970 monograph on comparative negligence, wrote that while contributory negligence was used as a defense as long ago as 1470, the comparative negligence concept—apportioning fault—was mentioned nearly a thousand years earlier in the Code of Justinian.

The concepts of liability and negligence developed pretty much on a case-by-case basis, defined as a particular judge or jury defined them. As early as 1500, wrote Henry Woods in his book *Comparative Fault*, a defendant in a personal injury case was usually held to be liable if the plaintiff could prove "wrongful intent" on the part of the defendant. As liability law developed, however, the element of negligence began approaching the element of intent in terms of importance.

The modern version of what we now call contributory negligence was born in the industrial revolution. As a matter of fact, Lawrence M. Friedman wrote in his *A History of American Law*, all of "(t)he modern law of torts must be laid at the door of the industrial revolution, whose machines had a marvelous capacity for smashing the human body." Before 1800, he said, "torts were an insignificant branch of the law."

The industrial revolution produced vast quantities of many things, but for a time it appeared one of its most shocking by-products would be a society weighed down by an army of maimed and disabled workers. With the revolution, large factories and industrial complexes came to dominate what had been a more rural and slower-paced society. With the great increases in productivity made possible by both huge and small machines came the reality of industrial injury. Machines allowed marvelous things to happen, but they also caused terrible things to happen—bone crushing, finger, hand, arm and leg amputating, and often terrible, fatal things.

At first judges were reluctant to hold industries to traditional liability standards. The courts felt it was more important to preserve business capital to be used for new investments than to divert some of the profits earned to compensate victims of business negligence.

Since the industrial revolution occurred in England before it began in the United States, it was natural that problems and legal solutions to those problems took place first there as well. "Contributory negligence can be traced, as a doctrine, to an English case decided in 1809," Friedman wrote. "But it was rarely used before the 1850s. What happened in between was the rise of the railroads. Almost every leading case in tort law was connected . . . with this new and dreadful presence. In this first generation of tort law, the railroad was the prince of machines. . . . It was the key to economic development. It cleared an iron path through the wilderness. It bound cities together, and tied the farms to the city and the seaports. Yet, trains were also wild beasts; they roared through the countryside, killing livestock, setting fire to crops, smashing passengers, and freight."

The contributory negligence concept, Schwartz wrote, was a "welcome rule" to business during the industrial revolution. Somewhat novel defense arguments won judicial approval to give a legalistic coloration to a purely economic contention: that progress was necessary for society to prosper, that accidents were an inevitable price of progress, and that too rigid an application of the tort laws of the time could stifle that progress. Did the plaintiff in any way contribute to the accident? If so, no recovery. Was the plaintiff voluntarily placed in a position where he or she might be an accident victim? If so, no recovery. Was an injury caused by the negligence of a co-worker, instead of by the direct negligence of the business owner? If so, no recovery from the business owner, although the plaintiff was free to sue the co-worker if he or she wished.

The development of contributory negligence and similar arguments aimed at protecting business interests from liability was harsh for accident victims but "extraordinarily useful" for judges, Friedman says. "It became the favored method by which judges kept tort claims from the deliberations of the jury. The trouble with the jury was that pitiful cases of crippled men suing giant corporations worked on their sympathies. . . . Juries showed a deep-dyed tendency to forget the facts that favored the defendant, and find for the plaintiff in personal-injury cases. But if the plaintiff was clearly negligent himself, there could be no recovery, there were no facts to be found, and the case could be taken from the jury and dismissed."

Friedman cites a case in which a trial court judge kept a case from going to a jury and candidly laid out the economic rationale for his decision. A fire had broken out in a railroad yard in Syracuse, NY, through the "careless management" of an engine, and flying sparks had started fires in nearby residences, completely consuming several. One homeowner sued the railroad.

"There was no question that the railroad was at fault, that the fire was the product of negligence," Friedman writes. "But how much should the railroad pay? The court shrank in horror from the thought of liability to people in the position of the plaintiff." They had, after all, chosen to live next to a railroad yard, where fires were a possibility. They had voluntarily placed themselves in a position where they could be harmed by an accident stemming from negligence in the railroad yard.

"To sustain such a claim," Friedman quotes the court in *Ryan v. New York Central Railroad Company*, ". . . would subject (the railroad) to a liability against which no prudence could guard, and to meet which no private fortune could be adequate. To hold that the owner. . . must guarantee the security of his neighbors on both sides, and to an unlimited extent . . . would be the destruction of all civilized society. . . . In a commercial country, each man, to some extent, runs the hazard of his neighbor's conduct." The railroad was held not liable for the destruction caused by its negligence "precisely because the harm it caused was *too* great, even though the damage could clearly, morally, be laid at its door," Friedman concludes.

The legal concept used to deny the neighbors of the railroad yard compensation was called "assumption of the risk." In theory it stated that when an individual understood the danger and still took the risk, there would be no liability and no compensation in the event of an injury. The concept was an effective weapon in manufacturers' legal defense arsenal and was particularly useful in dealing with the efforts of injured workers to seek compensation. In practice it meant that every employee was deemed to have assumed nearly every possible risk involved in their employment by virtue of their decision to accept the job in the first place and to continue working.

An early New Jersey case demonstrates the kind of risks workers were deemed to have "assumed" simply because they needed a paycheck to support their families. In *Cetola v. Lehigh Valley Railroad Company*, Cetola, a salaried employee, was cutting rails for the railroad on January 17, 1916. He was told by a foreman to assist four other men who had lifted a 27-foot-long, 648-pound rail. He went to where the four men were struggling with the heavy rail, but before he was able to help, they dropped it and Cetola was seriously injured.

The court acknowledged that the work Cetola and other employees were asked to do was very dangerous. It nevertheless denied Cetola any compensation, holding that he had, simply by showing up at work, assumed the risk of being injured. Cetola, unable to work, became a public charge. The railroad continued to serve the public. Some of the public.

But as beneficial to the economic health of the time as the contributory negligence concept might have been, its patent unfairness to individual victims, many horribly and permanently maimed, nagged continually at the conscience of the judiciary. New, countering arguments were advanced by plaintiffs' lawyers, and some were accepted. Did the defendant have one last, clear chance to avoid causing the accident that resulted in injury? If he or she had the chance, and didn't take it, liability was established. Had the defendant observed safety precautions stated in the law, installing lights and bells at railroad crossings, for instance? If not, he or she could be liable for the injuries caused in a car-train collision.

Court after court in England and the United States, unable to stomach the blatant injustices being done, began pecking away at the virtual immunity railroads and manufacturing firms had acquired from liability for injuries they caused. A major factor in the return to accountability was the distressingly drastic increase in accidents and injuries caused by industrial equipment and the practices of employers because the need to consider safety had been removed by the deference paid to the contributory negligence doctrine. As the body count of victims thrown aside without any compensation mounted, there developed the dramatically different concept that employers had a responsibility to provide a safe workplace.

As courts slowly overcame their reluctance to allow injured workers to recover compensation, the industrial barons went into their first panic over potential accountability. The specter of being hauled into court and forced to compensate workers for injuries caused by unsafe conditions prompted manufacturers to begin searching for any remedy that would allow them to avoid full accountability. What they accepted, reluctantly, was the beginnings of what we now call the worker's compensation system.

Although attempts to create a form of worker's compensation were made as early as 1917, modern worker's compensation laws were a product of the 1930s. Prior to their enactment, an injured worker was in the legal limbo of a changing system. While courts were beginning to allow recovery for industrial accidents, it was first necessary to prove negligence on the part of the employer. That was rarely difficult, since concern over workplace safety had been virtually ignored for decades, but the injured workers faced practical problems of a pressing nature. With income stopped and medical bills mounting without any immediate source of payment, a permanently injured worker soon was found in unbelievable financial straits. He or she couldn't wait out the lengthy legal process necessary to prove negligence.

As increasingly more powerful labor unions illustrated the upsurge in workers' strength across the country, there was a strong demand for the right to rapid and full compensation if a worker were injured on the job. Seeing the handwriting on the wall, manufacturers were quick to strike a deal that would both severely limit their accountability for the injuries resulting from their factories, and allow them to pass along a good portion of the costs of that compensation to the very employees themselves.

The new system provided benefits to any covered worker

who was injured on the job. An employee who was injured on the job because of his or her own carelessness or inattention was in the same boat, and received the same benefits, as someone who was an innocent victim of someone else's negligence. In addition to being a certain thing, the benefits were paid quickly—obviously of importance to workers whose low or moderate incomes prevented the accumulation of substantial savings.

Most employers were required to have insurance coverage to take care of this new workers' right to automatic compensation, and most employers immediately added the cost of that insurance into the workers "benefits" column, effectively requiring employees to pay for worker's compensation insurance out of their own salaries.

While workers receive at least the promise of automatic and rapid compensation, employers succeeded in severely limiting the amount of compensation. For instance, only a percentage of the worker's full wages are paid while he or she is off work due to industrial injury or disability. Any difference between the full wage and the temporary disability rate is simply lost to the worker. The top compensation rate paid by the California system in 1989 was $5.60 per hour, or $224 a week. If a worker had been earning more than that and had run up bills based on anticipation of that higher income, too bad. Under the worker's compensation system, the most personal and real harm caused by an industrial injury—the daily pain, the lifetime of suffering caused by a lost hand or shattered kneecap, and the profound deterioration in the enjoyment of life caused by a serious industrial accident—is not compensated at all.

It should be noted that even though the benefits are supposed to be automatic, arguments still occur as to whether the worker is actually injured, and if so, whether the injury was job-related. In addition, there can be and frequently are disagreements over the severity of the injury, and how disabling it is. If a worker is prevented from performing the job he or she spent 20 years learning by an industrial injury, but is not incapacitated from performing some other, perhaps less strenuous but lower-paying job, then the worker is entitled only to partial disability while the new job is being learned. Also, only injuries which affect ability to work are compensable. For instance, if continued exposure at work to toxic substances prevents an employee from ever having children, the employee would get not a dime of compensation unless it could be proven that the resulting psychological damage affected his or her ability to work.

With the creation of the worker's compensation system, industrial accident victims were finally treated more fairly, but the concept of contributory negligence survived in most American states for many more decades. Compensation to many victims not covered by worker's compensation was still denied.

The obvious unfairness caused by the contributory negligence rule was dealt with effectively and efficiently in Mississippi as early as 1910, where the legislature simply abolished it and substituted a system of comparative negligence. England abolished the contributory negligence rule in 1945, but 30 years and hundreds of thousands of uncompensated victims later, it was still the rule of law in California.

It might still be the law in California had Nga Li not decided her Oldsmobile needed some gas on Nov. 21, 1968, and turned left on Alvarado Street. "It wasn't a particularly complicated case, but it took a long time before it was decided because it asked that a drastic change in the law be made," Nga Li's attorney, Joseph E. Hall, recalls. "I knew my client's father, and that's how I became involved. I took the case on contingency, but I knew there wasn't much money that was going to be made on it. The principle—having the comparative negligence concept replace contributory negligence—made it intriguing. Turned out I didn't make any money on the case at all, nor did my client. After the Supreme Court overturned the Superior Court judge's decision, but before the case went to trial again, Yellow Cab went broke."

9

A SELF-MADE CRISIS

On May 11, 1970, Michael Egan, 55, was hard at work doing what he had done for most of his adult life: building roofs in the growing community of Pomona, California. Only on this day, as he stepped from a roof onto a ladder, a rung broke out from under him and sent him sprawling 12 feet to the ground, severely injuring his back and preventing him from working.

Fortunately, Michael Egan had had the foresight to buy a disability policy from Mutual of Omaha. It paid him $200 per month in the event of a disabling injury, and the insurance company dutifully made the payments—until it became clear that he was not going to recover. Suddenly, Mutual of Omaha decided that Egan's disability was caused by sickness, not by injury, and stopped the monthly payments. Sounds like the tactic used by U.L. Fletcher's insurance company, doesn't it?

Like U.L. Fletcher, Michael Egan had worked hard all his life, had had the foresight to buy a disability insurance policy, and wasn't about to cave in to an insurance company trying to stiff him. He went to see William Shernoff, a Pomona lawyer, and filed suit. At the trial, Shernoff forced Mutual of Omaha to produce its files relating to Egan's case and proved that the company had changed the status of Egan's disability from accident-caused to sickness-caused for the express purpose of saving money. An outraged jury awarded Egan his full disability, $78,000, and added $5 million in punitive damages.

Mutual of Omaha appealed, all the way to the California Supreme Court. The Court said that Mutual of Omaha had acted in bad faith in its conduct toward Michael Egan, and upheld the $78,000 award. It agreed that punitive damages were justified, but felt that $5 million was too severe. It sent the question of the punitive damage award back for another jury to determine. Mutual of Omaha elected to settle rather than risk having another jury decide an appropriate punishment. One condition of the settlement was that the amount remain confidential.

The Fletcher case had already sent shock waves through the insurance industry, and the Egan case intensified them. The cases set in motion the events that would move the industry into the forefront of the assault on consumer rights.

It may be difficult to believe, in view of the zeal of the insurance industry's continuing campaign against the civil justice system, but the two once had a healthy, mutually beneficial relationship. When members of the business community became aware that the civil justice system was going to hold them accountable for injuries they had caused, they demanded insurance against being held liable. Liability, or, as it's sometimes called, casualty insurance, is the kind of insurance we all purchase to provide coverage in the unfortunate event that we cause someone harm. Homeowners buy it in case a visitor trips and falls and breaks an arm because of an uneven slab of cement on the walkway to the house. A business obtains liability coverage in case someone is injured because a purchased product or service was deficient. Liability coverage is literally the stepchild of tort law, and has grown and developed as an industry with the growth and maturity of the civil justice system. Quite simply, without legal accountability, there would be no need for liability insurance.

For a while, the insurance companies enjoyed a no-lose situation. The developing tort law created the opportunity for companies to sell policies to the newly accountable members of what was becoming the defense lobby, and the companies dutifully defended their clients in court and paid claims when necessary. As long as they ran their businesses conservatively and aggressively represented their clients, all was well. But eventually, courts began to hold insurance companies themselves accountable for their actions, and their role as detached middlemen began to change.

The Fletcher and Egan cases, and others like them, made insurance companies defendants instead of simply the representatives of defendants. They began to identify more and more with the defendants they had represented, soon becoming active members of the defense lobby in its campaign to turn back the legal clock.

Even as tort law was providing valuable expanding markets for casualty insurance to grow, an underlying tension had developed. The emergence of true accountability under the law made selling insurance easier and more profitable, but it also made more certain the eventuality of having to pay claims. The business of selling insurance and the business of paying claims created a kind of institutional schizophrenia. In and of itself, the conflict was understandable and manageable. But beginning in the early 1970s, the world of insurance began to undergo another change, one that would have far-reaching consequences both for insurance consumers and for the civil justice system.

Slowly, and without much attention, the insurance industry shifted its primary emphasis from that of underwriting risk to that of high finance. Exciting new opportunities for insurance companies had begun appearing in the late '60s, when the U.S. economy started leaving the days of stable interest rates and conservative stock prices and entered a much more volatile investment climate. The firms soon discovered the vast assets they had accumulated over the decades could be turned to fast and often staggering profits through short-term investment.

A new and more profound schizophrenia overtook the industry. The business of insurance had suddenly become two separate and distinct enterprises existing within the same corporate shell: an underwriting business concerned with the traditional insurance chores of calculating risks, marketing insurance, and paying claims; and an investment business concerned with maximizing profits on its investment portfolio.

At first the two enterprises coexisted in an uneasy symbiotic relationship. Through insurance premiums, the underwriting side of the business provided a steady infusion of money for the investment side to operate with. But the two businesses operated under entirely different principles and were affected by entirely different economic factors within the marketplace.

Underwriting, the traditional role of insurance, is a simple, traditional business operation. It is based on the law of large numbers—the cost of paying claims can be spread among ever-increasing numbers of policyholders—providing a sense of security to all insurance purchasers and a healthy profit to the insurance company. Profit results when the money collected in premiums is greater than the costs of paying claims and operating the business, and that—taking in more than was paid out—was how insurance companies made their money until 15 or 20 years ago.

The income part of the business—revenue from premiums—is easy enough to understand. It's the cost part that gets tricky. Insurance costs include all the obvious: agents' commissions, the salaries and expenses of claims adjusters and administration, and of course the cost of claims actually paid. But costs also include payments into a sizable category labeled "reserves." Reserves are by nature speculative. They include those claims that have already been made but for which no payment has yet been made, as well as estimates of how much money will eventually be paid out on claims that have not even been made yet. If the reserves, both known and estimated, combined with all the other known costs exceed the premiums collected, the insurance company has an "underwriting loss." To most people, that would mean the company lost money, but in the world of insurance it means no such thing.

Companies complain that underwriting performance has gone from earning a profit in 1971 to incurring a loss in 1985. That may be true, although there are independent analysts who don't believe it. They contend that vast sums of money are brought in annually in premiums ($160 billion in 1986 alone), and while companies are loathe to open their books, analysts insist less than half the premiums collected each year are eventually paid out in claims and expenses. The rest of the money goes into the firms' reserves and is invested.

Despite what the insurance industry would have us believe, the underwriting portion of the business is relatively stable. Even major weather disasters over time have proven to fit neatly into the actuarial calculations so that catastrophic events (events that cause more than $5 million in insured loss) are already factored into the base rate premiums written.

As we learned in the tragic 1989 earthquake in Northern California, the companies have learned to limit or eliminate their loss from these types of catastrophes. Many of the companies wrote their earthquake coverage in such a way that the deductible was a percentage of the total value of the property, not a percentage of the loss. For instance, if a property owner had a $200,000 home (common in San Francisco) and the earthquake deductible was 15 percent, that deductible would be $30,000, no matter what the actual loss was. If the home suffered $29,000 in damage, the insured person could not collect a dime from the insurance company.

But even if the analysts are wrong and the companies are correct in stating they are suffering underwriting losses, it is a consequence of a decision made by the companies themselves. Over the same 14-year period during which, insurance companies said, their underwriting ventures went from black ink to red, their investment income rose from $2 billion to more than $25 billion. "Losing money" in the underwriting portion of the insurance business is literally a cost of doing the more lucrative investment business, for the gains made in the investment markets more than make up for the paper underwriting losses.

Because of this, premiums paid by consumers are no longer driven by actuarial considerations of costs and claims, but by the cyclical nature of the investment industry. In order to have money available to invest when interest rates are high and investment opportunities are attractive, companies are quite willing to price policies low enough to attract business and bring in premiums even though they know the income from the premiums will not be sufficient to pay off claims.

In short, the top priority of the companies is no longer insurance, it is investment, and insurance is merely a means to that end. The headlong rush to collect investment dollars sometimes is carried to startling lengths. For example, in the months following the MGM Grand Hotel fire in Las Vegas a few years ago, an insurance consortium was put together AFTER the fire to cover the losses and MGM paid a premium for this "coverage." Some would ask how "insurance" can be sold to cover a loss after the loss has occurred. The answer is the consortium expected the earnings from investing the substantial MGM premium would exceed the payout on the policy.

Insurance companies have tremendous flexibility in terms of setting premium levels and reporting losses. In essence, they are free to price their product at any level, either under- or over-report losses at will, and do it individually or collectively, since the insurance industry is exempt from the antitrust laws that bind every other business in the country except some professional sports.

There are, however, two major structural constraints with which the industry has always had to contend. The first is the network of state regulatory systems. In general, state regulation of insurance companies is directed solely at monitoring gross financial data to ensure solvency. Most states require insurance companies to maintain surplus funds to act as a cushion in the event the company's reserve accounts become inadequate. This surplus account acts to limit the amount of insurance policies a company can write. As a general rule, insurance companies are required to maintain a written premium-to-surplus ratio of between 2:1 and 3:1. For example, in order for an insurance company to write and collect $30 million in premiums, it should have $15 million in its surplus account and is not permitted to have less than $10 million.

The second structural constraint is that the normal rules of supply and demand are, in one respect, seriously distorted in the insurance industry. Demand in the insurance industry is relatively static. Everyone needs insurance, but a glut in supply does not itself create a need or desire for additional insurance. Color television sets selling for $50 might create a demand for a second or even a third color set in a household, but once you have insured your car and house, and are signed up for life insurance and a decent health care plan, there is little need for a second or third insurance policy,

119

regardless of price.

The "supply," in insurance, is money. Since profits in the insurance business have come almost exclusively from the investment side of the business for the past 15 to 20 years, when highly profitable investment opportunities arise, big-time investors flock to the industry since insurance is a relatively safe source of substantial returns. This is because, according to state premium-to-surplus requirements, every $10 million in surplus capital can bring in $20 million to $30 million worth of premiums to invest. As a result, the supply (new capital) is highly volatile, increasing dramatically as investment opportunities become more attractive and decreasing equally dramatically as investment profits deteriorate.

Consequently, despite the static demand, when attractive investment opportunities appear, fierce competition takes place among individual companies for market share. During this period, sound underwriting practices are abandoned, premiums are cut in order to be competitive, and underwriting losses begin to grow. The profits made in the investment market are used both to "cover" the investment losses and to support even further competition.

Eventually, losses for all the expanded coverages written at bargain basement prices begin to pile up. In the normal insurance cycle, the competitive phase will drive profits down industry-wide to the point where the damage becomes too great and the market begins to turn. Unfortunately, in a cycle driven by particularly attractive investment opportunities, the competitive phase tends to last as long as the investment opportunities last, and the resulting damage to industry finances is exaggerated. If the investment market takes a sudden downturn during the competitive phase when high investment returns are being counted on to compensate for increasing underwriting losses, the results can be devastating.

That is exactly what happened during the "insurance crises" of both the mid-70s and the mid-80s. In the early 1970s, the stock market was reaching record highs. The liability insurance companies engaged in a brief but intense competition, cutting premiums, particularly in "long-tail" lines such as medical malpractice, and deliberately depleting their reserves. In February 1973, the Dow Jones Industrial Average reached an all-time high of 1100, but by the end of May it had fallen to 580, and the competitive phase of that insurance cycle came to a crashing halt. The sudden drop in stock prices eliminated much of the investment income the companies had counted on to bail out the underpriced underwriting side of their business. As a result, they took the only other option open to them— they raised premiums astronomically and canceled some lines of insurance—and a "crisis" developed.

The scenario was repeated in the '80s. Investment opportunities abounded, and ignoring all the lessons of the past, companies again undermined their own financial security by depleting their reserves and incurring immense claims obligations beyond their ability to pay in frenetic get-rich-now plunges. Early in 1984, members of the insurance industry became aware that substantial trouble was brewing. Ignoring all the lessons of the past and frantically undermining their own financial security, companies had depleted their reserves and incurred immense claims obligations beyond their capacity to pay in a freewheeling investment-driven, get-rich-now scheme. By mid-1984 it was clear a crash was coming and the result would be a massive dislocation and financial retrenchment within the industry that would affect virtually every consumer of liability insurance in the country. As in 1973, insurance companies would find themselves in another "crisis" and again be forced to jack up premiums and abandon selected lines of insurance.

The political heat that would result from this second round of widespread policy cancellations and skyrocketing premiums was likely to end once and for all the industry's privileged position as the last virtually unregulated financial goliath.

The industry had a strategy, however; it had worked once, and figured to work again. Some of the biggest premium increases during the insurance crisis of the '70s had occurred in medical malpractice insurance, but the industry diverted responsibility by blaming the price hikes on the civil justice system. That strategy paid off in spades for the insurers with the passage of the fore-runner of much of the "tort reform" that has subsequently plagued the country, the Medical Injury Compensation Reform Act of 1975 (MICRA), which limited the sizes of awards and contingency fees.

The tactic succeeded even though no substantive evidence was ever produced demonstrating any link between the civil justice system and the price hikes in medical malpractice insurance. As a matter of fact, a large group of Southern California doctors hired William Shernoff to sue the insurance companies for a return of overcharged premiums, and he succeeded in getting more than $40 million returned to them.

The industry remembered the diversion strategy in 1984, and once again launched an attack on the civil justice system in an effort to shift attention from its own sins and to pressure legislators into taking away consumers' rights for the greater good of lower insurance rates. In December of 1984 the industry newspaper, *National Underwriter,* reported that the Insurance Information Institute, insurance's political arm, had announced the need for a massive effort to "... market the idea there is something wrong with the civil justice system in the United States."

Notice the words chosen: "... *market* the idea." They might well have been trying to sell a new mouthwash. Then there's "... something wrong ... ," not anything in particular; let's not get so specific we can be proven wrong. Just cry wolf, and cry wolf loudly, the Institute urged.

Shortly after the rallying cry had been sounded, the Insurance Information Institute devoted $6.5 million to an advertising campaign trying to change the perception of the impending insurance crisis to that of a "lawsuit crisis." The myth of the litigation explosion was repeated constantly as the industry attempted to divert attention away from the real reason for the drastic swings between periods of reasonably priced and readily available coverages and periods of dramatically increasing premiums and severe availability problems.

With the insurance crisis of 1984, the insurance industry moved to the front in the war against consumer rights, and the battle took on a considerably more vicious tone. To hide the blunders of the industry in the creation of a marketplace where insurance was either too expensive or simply not available, considerably more than ordinary diversions were called for. As the campaign of distortion and misdirection was played out, insurers raised premium rates to unheard-of highs, and blamed it on the civil justice system. They canceled policies for cities and counties large and small because they did not have the capital to support the insurance, and blamed it on the civil justice system. They abandoned some markets—child care was dropped completely, even though later studies proved that child care centers had paid in vastly more premiums than had ever gone out to pay for claims—and blamed it on the civil justice system.

Increasingly, the original purpose for the existence of insurance companies—handling claims for damages or losses or liability of any sort—was viewed by the industry as an affront not to be tolerated; the consuming public was characterized as either instigators of fraudulent claims or members of wild-eyed juries; lawyers, both plaintiff and defense, were castigated as serving no purpose other than to drain insurers' investment resources; and the civil justice system itself was seen as an irritant rather than an institution developed through the centuries as a civilized method of settling disputes fairly and peaceably.

Horror stories, depicting just how crazy the civil justice system had become, began appearing in speeches and press releases across the country. Some of the horror stories were repeated so often they became familiar.

Surely, for instance, you've read or heard about the burglar who fell through a skylight on a school roof and was awarded $260,000. That case never even went to trial; it was settled, the story goes. The real story, as told by the mother of the victim in testimony to Congress:

"In February of 1982, Ricky and three of his companions climbed to the roof of Enterprise High School to remove an outdoor light located on the roof. The boys planned to take the light and use it to light their makeshift basketball court.

"Ricky stepped through a skylight which had been covered by tar by the school district. Ricky fell through the skylight, landing on the gymnasium floor below and suffering severe brain damage.

"Ricky was in a coma for seven months following the accident. Though doctors said it was likely he would never come out of the coma, he has since regained consciousness and is beginning physical rehabilitation. Ricky currently has no use of his legs or of one arm. He also lost all power of speech, though we hope it can be regained. Although Ricky has been progressing, he requires constant care.

"In all the articles written about my son, I have yet to read anything about the school's responsibility in this instance. Granted, what Ricky did was wrong, as he would be the first to admit. He was 18 years old and it was a stupid prank for which he is paying a very high price. But does this absolve the responsibility of the school district?

"A boy was killed in nearby Shasta High a year before Rick's accident. He fell through the school's gym skylight, as did Rick at Enterprise High. These skylights were ordered replaced, but

Enterprise High School chose to ignore the order to eliminate the skylight and painted over it with tar, making it virtually impossible to tell from the rest of the roof.

"I would also like to point out that it was with the full knowledge of school authorities that students were climbing on the roof constantly to retrieve balls, etc. It could have been anyone of them or even a workman who unsuspectingly stepped on the skylight.

"Having this knowledge and knowing of the potential danger involved, why didn't the school authorities take steps to prevent this from happening? Especially after the death of the young man from Shasta High School.

"How many tragedies does it take for people in positions of authority to take action? Given the school's knowledge of what happened at Shasta High, its knowledge that kids did use its roof, and its failure to comply with the order to remove the skylight, I think you will agree that the school was negligent and that negligence played a major role in bringing about my son's injury."

Assistant U.S. Attorney General Richard Willard used the "Burglar gets $260,000" often, even after the testimony of Ricky's mother. Another Willard story, as reported in the *Washington Post*, went as follows:

"He (Willard) cited a 1979 case of a 16-year-old girl who was injured when the drunk driver of the car she was riding in ran a stop sign, and the car collided with another. The City of Los Angeles was found to be 22 percent liable due to poor visibility of the street lane lines. . . ."

The real story was somewhat different. Kathy Sills was being driven home by a friend during a rainy night. The accident occurred when the driver missed seeing a stop sign and was hit by a pick-up truck. Tests registered no blood alcohol in the driver. The intersection was extremely dangerous in that there was no "stop ahead" sign, no markings whatsoever on the roadway to indicate where a stop should be made, and the city had allowed debris and trees to cover the single existing stop sign so that it was almost completely obscured from vision.

Even CBS's venerable "60 Minutes" joined the fray and showed a segment containing some of the classic horror stories. In January 1988, however, "60 Minutes" ran a segment titled "Re-Examination of Lawsuit Crisis." What follows is a partial transcript from that show:

ED BRADLEY: "The insurance industry says we're in the midst of a giant lawsuit crisis. And on the face of it, they make a pretty good case. We've all heard of crazy lawsuits and outrageous jury awards.... The insurance industry thinks that's ridiculous and wants states to put limits on jury awards. Recently they made a series of commercials that say the lawsuit crisis is even worse than you might imagine."

ANNOUNCER: "One out of nine obstetricians surveyed has stopped delivering babies. Some mothers have had to find new doctors. Others have had to travel elsewhere to give birth. It's part of the lawsuit crisis."

ANNOUNCER: "Today schools are thinking about canceling football and other major sports. It's part of the lawsuit crisis."

ANNOUNCER: "Our cities are in a bind. Money needed for firefighters, police, and other services is being used to pay the price of the lawsuit crisis. New York City says lawsuits may soon cost as much as the Fire Department."

BRADLEY: "Well, what about it? For openers, leading experts on manpower shortages in medicine tell us lawsuits are causing no shortage of obstetrical services now, nor will they in the foreseeable future.

"About high school sports.For the last seven years we've found just six successful lawsuits against schools' sports programs.

In other words, less than once a year one school's sports program, one out of 20,000 throughout America, pays out on a lawsuit.

"And what about those threatened city services? A New York City official did once say that lawsuits may soon cost as much as the city's fire department. But he doesn't say it anymore. It was, his office admitted, an overstatement. Last year, for every dollar the city spent to settle legal claims, it spent more than four dollars for fire protection.

"This magazine ad is also part of the insurance industry campaign. It says clergymen are being sued because of their advice. Well, it's hardly a crisis. It's happened twice, and not one penny had been paid because a pastor gave a parishioner a bum steer."

Bradley then discussed a horror story with which Californians were particularly familiar. The story took place in the Los Angeles suburb of Inglewood.

BRADLEY: "But what about the stories of plaintiffs who have gotten huge awards? Charles Bigbee was in a phone booth hit by an allegedly drunk driver.

"All of the time you saw the car coming towards you?"

CHARLES BIGBEE: "I saw it coming towards me. Yes, sir. The angle that she hit the phone booth forced the glass inward, and it just chewed my leg off right there at the spot."

BRADLEY: "The glass cut your leg off?"

BIGBEE: "Cut it right off."

BRADLEY: "Bigbee sued the driver and the phone company. When the California Supreme Court said he was entitled to a jury trial, President Reagan had one of his favorite lawsuit stories."

PRESIDENT REAGAN: "According to Chief Justice Rose Bird of the California Supreme Court, a jury could find that the companies responsible for the design, location, installation, and maintenance of the telephone booth were liable. I suppose this might be amusing if such absurd results only took place occasionally. Yet

127

today they have become all but commonplace."

BRADLEY: "Cruz Reynoso is a former California Supreme Court Justice, one of the six justices, six out of seven, who said Bigbee was entitled to a jury trial."

CRUZ REYNOSO: "What the president has done is to take a case and dramatize it by leaving out a great many of the facts that are involved, and therefore putting it in a context that appears to be silly. Important in this matter and not mentioned by the president, was that there had been a previous accident at precisely the same site with precisely the same booth."

BRADLEY: "The possibility that the booth had been placed in an unsafe location wasn't the only thing the president failed to mention."

(To Bigbee) "What happened when you tried to open the door?"

BIGBEE: "When I tried to open the door it would not open."

BRADLEY: "According to the sworn testimony of an eyewitness, that is exactly what happened. He said that the last thing he saw Mr. Bigbee doing was pulling at the door, struggling to get out. That was just before the car impacted and hit the phone booth."

BRADLEY: "You're aware of what President Reagan said about your case."

BIGBEE: "They're saying that my case is outrageous. But he doesn't tell 'em that the phone booth had been struck before. He doesn't tell 'em I was stuck in the phone booth. He doesn't tell 'em I had to stand there and just get run over like an animal. He doesn't say all that."

The lie had been exposed, but the damage was already being done. The period from 1985 through 1987 was a disastrous one for consumer rights in statehouses across the country. Consumers' rights to full compensation for injuries caused by negligence were limited in Alabama, Georgia, Idaho, Kansas, Oregon, Texas, Utah,

Virginia, and Washington. Significant procedural changes that effectively reduce the compensation owed to an innocent victim were passed in Alaska, Arizona, California, Idaho, Louisiana, Missouri, Montana, Nevada, North Dakota, Ohio, Oregon, South Dakota, Texas, and Washington. In virtually every state, consumers were on the defensive trying to withstand one of the most concerted and vicious attacks on consumers' and victims' rights ever witnessed.

Perhaps the most blatant exercise of raw self-interest by the insurance industry occurred in California in 1988, when the industry spent more than $74 million trying to persuade voters to insulate the industry from risk. That is more money than has ever been spent by a single interest in an election, excepting only national presidential elections. The industry wanted to impose a particularly pernicious form of no-fault automobile insurance to enable them to avoid paying many of the benefits insurers now offer, without a reduction in premiums. They wanted to establish in law that insurance companies were exempt from the same price-fixing prohibitions and anti-trust regulations to which virtually every other industry is subject. They wanted to be free from government involvement in the rate-setting process, despite the fact that automobile insurance is mandated by law in California and other kinds of insurance are economic necessities for most people. And they wanted to lock the door of the courthouse to persons complaining of grievances against them by removing the incentive for successful lawyers to represent less-than-wealthy victims.

Think about that $74 million expenditure in California for a moment. Clearly, the insurance industry viewed that $74 million as a business investment—a contingency investment, if you will—that would have been returned many times over if the campaign had been successful. Happily for California consumers, it wasn't.

The lure that prompted that incredible 1988 investment in

129

California is still there, however. And so, the assualt on consumer rights continues. Insurance is no longer the business of spreading risks and settling claims, and the courthouse is no longer the main focus of dispute resolution. Insurance today is the business of big investments, and all other considerations—including justice—are secondary. In short, the insurance industry has lost its way.

10

THE HIGH COST OF
NO FAULT

To the accompaniment of the reverberating sound of the insurance crash of 1984, the insurance industry moved out of the ranks of the neutral parties and into the front lines in the war against consumer rights. What started as a panicked attempt to divert blame from itself for the nationwide insurance mess quickly became the equivalent of a holy crusade.

The insurance industry had grown powerful as a service adjunct to the civil justice system. The civil justice system would hold a wrongdoer accountable; and an insurance company, by spreading the liability risk over a large number of policyholders, could assure the victim would be compensated and the wrongdoer would not be financially ruined. But as the rules of accountability began to be applied to the insurance industry itself, and as lucrative investment possibilities overcame the industry's more conservative reliance on underwriting profits, the civil justice system became an irritant rather than an opportunity.

The insurance industry no longer needed to serve the civil justice system. In fact, it was now committed to doing away with the system completely, or at least making it inaccessible to anyone whose successful use of it might reduce the capital available for investment. In its vision of the ideal world, the insurance industry itself would take over control of the administrations of justice. It would decide if someone were injured, and how much, if any, compensation should be paid. One of its earliest campaigns in the newly escalated war was a nationwide effort to enact no-fault automobile insurance.

Society, speaking through developments in tort law, has determined that each of us has a responsibility to avoid causing injury to another person. In legal language, this is called a duty of due care. That responsibility is placed on all of us, whether we are individuals, corporations, or governments. When an insurance company violates its duty of due care to an insured, a manufacturing firm violates its responsibility toward a purchaser of its products, a government breaches its duty to a citizen, or an individual's carelessness results in an injury to another; then society, through its responsibility-based civil justice system, holds the wrongdoer accountable.

Hold that thought for a minute: The party responsible for injuries to someone else is held accountable for the consequences of those injuries! Hardly a new concept, as I think I've demonstrated, but apparently a concept some think has outlived its usefulness.

In its stead, the insurance industry has decided to advocate an alternative method of compensating society's injured victims: "no-fault." In a no-fault system, the only requirement is that there be an injury. Whether the injured person caused the accident or was a victim of another's negligence makes no difference. Although there are many types of no-fault and the variations seem endless, the concept in each is the same. If you are injured in an accident you are entitled to compensation, regardless of whose fault it is. If you caused that accident you get the same compensation as the person you injured. The issue of responsibility, of fault, does not come into the equation.

In fact, no-fault mocks the very concept of responsibility. For example, since the theory of automobile no-fault insurance is that everyone should be compensated, regardless of whether he or she were the innocent victim or the negligent driver, it has the obvious potential for doubling the total number of compensated persons. The insurance industry is in favor of such a system because increased claims means increases in auto insurance premiums.

In order to avoid the obviously politically impossible task of convincing anyone to accept a big increase in their auto premiums in order to compensate negligent drivers, no-fault includes a shell game within its structure. Innocent drivers (at least all but the most seriously injured) are no longer compensated for their pain and suffering as a result of an accident. The practical result is that compensation for the innocent victim is reduced and the amount saved is given instead to the negligent driver who caused the injuries in the first place.

The concept of no-fault was not an invention of insurance executives. It arose some 20 years ago, as an academic theory. Soon afterwards the theory was brought into the political arena and began to be debated publicly. The earliest concept was no-fault insurance across the board with respect to all injuries to all people, whether working or not, whether negligent or not. In theory, since everyone was going to get compensation, there wouldn't be so many arguments and thus that portion of the insurance dollar used for litigation and other administrative purposes would diminish and more funds would be available to compensate more victims more quickly. Even though the idea of abandoning the concepts of accountability and personal responsibility were troublesome to most people, the allure of saving money was enough to warrant experimentation.

During the early 1970s a number of states across the country adopted a no-fault automobile insurance system. Among the first was Massachusetts, where automobile insurance rates were among the highest in the country. Insurance interests argued that by eliminating the "small case" from the system—that is, injuries incurring medical expenses below a specified amount—great savings could be had and a more fair and universal method of compensation would result.

Furthermore, they said, if this "more efficient" system could be installed, lower insurance premiums would result. Massachusetts put the system in place in 1972 with this promise, and almost every state that followed Massachusetts and enacted no-fault did so with great fanfare and promises of premium reductions. Not only did premium prices not decrease, they kept right on increasing. Today, the automobile insurance rates in Massachusetts remain among the highest in the country. The cry now is that the system in place in Massachusetts is not an efficient no-fault system and should be changed to a better one.

The same scenario was played out in Nevada, where in the early 1970s a system of no-fault similar to the one in Massachusetts was installed. When insurance rates did not come down as a result of no-fault, the Nevada Legislature was again assured by the insurance industry that if it simply adopted a better no-fault system, lower rates would occur. The no-fault system in Nevada was changed, the rates did not come down, and the Legislature subsequently abolished the system altogether and returned Nevada to a concept based on the traditional values of responsibility. Pennsylvania has also tried no-fault and repealed it after it failed. Indeed, no state has adopted the system since 1976, although many, including California, are currently weathering intensive campaigns by the insurance industry to get no-fault enacted.

After the first heady days of no-fault experimentation resulted in rising premiums, under-compensated victims, and bureaucratic failures, the cry for no-fault was not heard across the country; although proponents in two states, New York and Florida, claimed that the version of no-fault they had adopted was working. In those states the level of benefits available to an injured person under the no-fault concept was limited and the ceiling for expenses covered under the system was fairly high. While originally conceived as taking only the small cases out of the system, in New York the no-fault system covered all accident victims unless bones were broken, the injured person was totally prevented from working for a very significant period of time, or there was a permanent injury of some kind. An individual who was prevented from working for 30 days and ran up $10,000 or $15,000 dollars in medical bills, but was then able to go back to work although still hurting, was within the no-fault system and could collect only the medical and wage loss benefits allowed under the system. This, it was promised, would certainly lower insurance rates.

It didn't. According to the New York State Department of Insurance, over the past several years insurance rates have not come down but rather have increased at about five percent a year. Florida's experience has been similar, but both New York and Florida would undoubtedly have seen much greater increases were it not for the fact that the insurance commissioner's offices in the two states, unlike their counterparts in other states, have considerable regulatory authority and were able to prevent bigger premium hikes.

Ironically, it was the very failure of no-fault to keep premiums down that attracted such strong support from the insurance industry. The closer companies looked at the system, the better it looked for them. The reason was simple: They could decide who got coverage and who didn't. They could decide who got paid, how much, and when. They could decide everything. By eliminating fault they could largely circumvent the civil justice system. By eliminating any liability for pain and suffering damages except in the most serious cases, they could eliminate the economic ability of victims to hire attorneys. By promising to pay everyone who was injured at least some compensation they would be "forced" to raise premiums. No-fault is an insurer's dream come true—high premiums with no tort law and no accountability.

Of course, theoretically, the system was still tied by thin threads to the courts. If, for example, an injured accident victim submitted $4,000 in medical bills and was told by the insurance company that it would only pay $2,000, theoretically, the courts were still available to settle that dispute. But practically, it made little difference. If injured policyholders who were denied all the benefits they thought they were entitled to were indignant enough to try to fight for the full benefits owed, they would undoubtedly go see an attorney. Just as undoubtedly the attorney would be forced to tell them that it did not really make economic sense to pursue their claim even though it was completely just.

Because no-fault restricts most benefit payments to a limited percentage of out-of-pocket losses, and completely eliminates any compensation for the pain and suffering of the victim, *any* amount of attorney fees would leave the poor victim at a loss. For example, if the attorney were paid by the hour it would cost at least $3,000 to recover the additional $2,000, and because of both the limited dollars involved and the fact that the client was certain to wind up with a net loss, few if any attorneys could take such cases on a contingency basis. The best any attorney could do would be to try to bluff the insurance company into increasing its offer. No-fault, as I said, is an insurer's dream.

In the face of numerous studies by the Rand Corporation which show that under the existing fault-based system the amount of compensation paid to people injured in automobile accidents had increased at approximately the same rate as inflation over the past 20 or 30 years, and the rate of lawsuits filed had increased at about the same rate as the population had increased, the insurance companies nevertheless began a campaign to sway public opinion against the existing responsibility-based method of compensating injured persons. The cry was the same as it has always been: "Greedy lawyers, victims who were exaggerating their injuries, wild juries and lenient judges" were about to bankrupt the insurance carriers that provided coverage for automobile accidents. Dusty concepts were spruced up and expensive public relations campaigns were begun.

But voters—as Californians demonstrated in 1988 when they defeated a no-fault initiative—were no longer willing to accept at face value the insurance industry's promises that lower rates would result from enactment of no-fault. As a matter of fact, midway through the 1988 campaign even the insurance companies gave up promising lower rates, and began to say only that the new system, if enacted, would result in a leveling off of rates and that the increases would be less substantial than they had been under the responsibility or fault-based system that had been in place for so many years. The tardy candor didn't help, and the industry-sponsored proposal, Proposition 104, received only 25 percent of the vote.

Despite the overwhelming rejection of no-fault, insurers urged a variation on the same scheme to California legislators when they went back to work early in 1989. Attempting to capitalize on the public outrage about skyrocketing insurance premiums, the insurers now argued that surrendering any claim to pain, suffering, and emotional distress damages in small automobile accident cases is a price society should be willing to pay for the promise of smaller increases in automobile insurance premiums.

However, the empirical evidence from across the country, including the studies discussed earlier, contradicts the insurers' contention that the "new" no-fault schemes would be sufficiently restrictive to control insurance rates. The basic problem is that although benefits are paid at a lower rate, they are paid to all who are injured, not just those who are innocent. So, the same amount of insurance dollars is being divided, or more, where rates have been raised, but those dollars are being divided among a greater number of people. More persons are compensated, but each with fewer dollars.

The question finally being asked is, how has the insurance companies' wealth been affected by no-fault, and what is the relationship between revenues received from premiums and investment of those premiums, and claims paid?

Led by the voters of California, consumers across the country are beginning to ask for full disclosure by the insurance companies of their internal costs and levels of profitability. That information generally had not been made available to lawmakers or the general public. The cry of "open your books and let us take a look" is heard now in many states across the country. The insurance industry has spent tens of millions of dollars trying to blame trial lawyers and the jury system for skyrocketing insurance rates, but a string of broken promises by the industry has finally focused the public's attention on where the responsibility for those rates rests: on the companies that set them, decline to explain how they do it, and refuse to divulge the profits they enjoy from premiums and investments.

What is happening to the public attitude, it seems, is a variation on an old maxim: The insurance companies fooled us once. Shame on them. If they fool us twice, shame on us!

11

THE JURY IN PERIL

Not all of the people in all of the states liked all of the provisions of the Constitution proposed for the new United States of America, Alexander Hamilton acknowledged in 1788. And not all of the citizens were satisfied that all of the necessary protections were in the document awaiting ratification.

But, Hamilton wrote in what has come to be known as *The Federalist:* "The friends and adversaries of the plan of the convention, if they agree in nothing else, concur at least in the value they set upon the trial by jury; or, if there is any difference between them it consists of this: the former regard it as a valuable safeguard to liberty; the latter represent it as the very palladium of free government."

Hamilton was correct, in 1788, in his assessment of the reverence held for the right to trial by jury, and his assessment was correct for some 180 years after the Constitution was ratified later that year. But his words wouldn't be true today. Not all the people agree that the trial by jury has value. More than that, some critics contend, trial by jury—or, specifically, trial by the people who are allowed to serve on juries—may be downright dangerous to the economic health of the United States.

And who are these critics?

Of course! The critics who don't like juries are the ones who can be hauled into court to face a jury when a citizen has become a victim. Not surprisingly, those interests who have been held accountable by juries and punished by juries don't like juries.

But the right to trial by jury is so fundamental an aspect of the American psyche that only the boldest of critics attack it directly. Instead, they attack lawyers, criticize judges, hammer at the process, all with the object of diminishing their own exposure to risk by preventing juries from hearing personal injury lawsuits. Fortunately, so far, they haven't gotten away with it. But they keep on trying.

"Essentially," syndicated columnist Murray Kempton wrote in 1986, "the war against the lawyers is at bottom a camouflaged aggression against the jury system. The offended covetous can always arraign lawyers for being covetous, but since jurors have no visible self-interest the worst that can be said of them is that they are foolish and sentimental. And yet, could any of the occasional awards, whose size now and then scandalized those of us who do not bother to find out the facts, have been rendered by any jury that had not lost its temper from the very shock of the defendant's mendacity and callousness?"

Richard J. Mahoney, chairman and chief executive officer of the Monsanto Company, is scandalized and boldly says so. "Conduct liable for punitive damages," he complained in a 1988 *New York Times* article, "is whatever a single jury says it is."

Author-engineer-lawyer Peter Huber, who has become perhaps the most quoted critic of our civil justice system, worries in his book , *Liability, The Legal Revolution and Its Consequences,* that jurors are intellectually inadequate for the responsibility they assume when they take their place in a courtroom. "(C)ould any jury really follow the wonderfully complex directions in any intelligent way?" Huber asks about citizens impaneled to hear a modern personal injury case.

The people pondering ratification of the Constitution may not have visualized today's complex, high-tech world, but their faith in the ability of ordinary citizens to hear evidence and reach a right conclusion was so strong that they insisted on an amendment guaranteeing the same right to trial by jury in civil cases that Article III, Section 2 provided for persons accused of having committed crimes.

Hamilton, in *The Federalist No. 83*, outlined the argument: "Hence, say they, as the Constitution has established the trial by jury in criminal cases, and is silent in respect to civil, this silence is an implied prohibition of trial by jury in regard to the latter." But that argument, he continued, is "contrary to reason and common sense, and therefore not admissable." There is an "inseparable connection between the existence of liberty, and the trial by jury in civil cases," and "(t)he strongest argument in its favor is that it is a security against corruption."

Hamilton, who opposed any action that would delay ratification, argued that the principle was so strongly embedded in the young nation's cultural composition that the addition of an amendment to the proposed Constitution specifically guaranteeing the right to trial by jury in civil cases was unnecessary. The ratifiers, however, particularly those in Massachusetts, were so fearful of abuses of the weak by the strong that they insisted on the guarantee's inclusion in the Bill of Rights.

Sir William Blackstone's *Commentaries* on English common law was about 20 years old at the time, and his discussion of the importance of the jury was undoubtedly cited by proponents of the Constitutional guarantee. The jury, Blackstone wrote, was the "bulwark of northern liberty" and "the glory of the English law." It was the institution best "adapted and framed for the investigation of truth."

Thomas Jefferson was obviously of like mind when, in a July 11, 1789, letter to Thomas Paine he expressed "apprehension" that a majority of the French National Assembly "cannot be induced to adopt the trial by jury; and I consider that as the only anchor ever yet imagined by man, by which a government can be held to the principles of its constitution."

It was essential that Americans be guaranteed this noble institution in the civil disputes as well as criminal trials, the ratifiers argued. They won the argument, and the Seventh Amendment reads: "In suits at common law, where the value in controversy shall exceed twenty dollars, the right of trial by jury shall be preserved, and no fact tried by a jury, shall be otherwise re-examined in any court of the United States, than according to the rules of the common law."

That language seems straightforward enough. The late U.S. Supreme Court Justice Hugo L. Black thought so. "It is my belief," Justice Black said in a 1960 lecture, "that there are 'absolutes' in our Bill of Rights, and that they were put there on purpose by men who knew what words meant."

Jury trial has been the means of determining guilt or innocence and resolving civil disputes for literally thousands of years. Lloyd E. Moore, in *The Jury*, wrote, "The ancient Mediterranean civilizations and the Germanic tribes had groups of laymen who participated in judgment."

There are 4,000-year-old references in Egyptian history to

the "kenbet," juries of four or eight citizens, half from one side of the Nile and half from the other, and the Greek poet-playwright Aeschylus, in *Eumenides*, dramatizes the trial by 12 Athenians of Orestes, who had been accused of slaying his mother, Clytemnestra.

History suggests, Moore writes, that the Romans adopted the jury form from the Greeks and carried it to Europe, and that the Normans took it with them when they conquered Great Britain in the 11th century. The Magna Charta, in 1215, guarantees judgment by the peers of an accused person, and there is continuing discussion among legal historians over whether the language refers to what we today would call civil matters as well as criminal ones.

Throughout history there have been examples of efforts to manipulate or flat-out direct juries to bring in a verdict desired by those in authority, and there have also been examples of courageous jurors ignoring the mandate and following their conscience.

Probably the most famous American example is the 1735 trial of John Peter Zenger, a New York newspaper publisher who was jailed and tried for his printed attacks on the colonial governor, William Cosby. Alexander Hamilton, representing Zenger, attempted to base his defense on the truth of Zenger's charges against Cosby. But the judge, a Cosby supporter, directed the jury to determine simply whether the charges had in fact appeared in print, reserving for himself the determination of whether the charges were libelous. Despite threats of being sent to jail themselves if they refused to follow the judge's orders, the jurors returned a unanimous verdict of not guilty, and the public acclaim forced the judge to free Zenger.

Modern-day critics of the jury system like to quote Mark Twain, who appeared to scorn the process in his 1872 reminiscence *Roughing It*. "The jury system," Twain wrote, very probably with his tongue planted firmly in his cheek, "puts a ban upon intelligence and honesty, and a premium upon ignorance, stupidity and perjury.

It is a shame that we must continue to use a worthless system because it was good a thousand years ago."

Distress with the right of plaintiffs in personal injury lawsuits to have juries hear their cases began developing in the 1960s. Leon Sarkey, writing in the *Loyola Law Review*, said civil jury trials ". . . represented the horse and buggy segment of the American administration of justice, reflecting a judicial provincialism and a mid-Victorian drag on our judicial process, which calls for realistic treatment by way of reform."

In *Liability*, Huber says simply that the ordinary people who comprise today's juries are not competent to cope with the complex issues presented them in most civil cases. Furthermore, he writes, the average juror brings to the courtroom a bias which should disqualify him or her from hearing most cases. "The inexpert juror is predisposed at every turn to identify the technologies that are novel, exotic, unfamiliar, or adventuresome as unwelcome and fraught with danger—in short, defective," Huber writes.

His book is laced with putdowns of Americans who serve on juries, usually in terms condescendingly suggesting that greedy plaintiffs and trial lawyers are to blame for placing these simpletons in trials where they are asked to do things they're not intellectually equipped to do. "(J)uries have often (and quite understandably) proved unskilled at distinguishing the various parties found at the scene of the crime," he writes. "They are too prone to arrest the firefighter along with the arsonist, the ambulance driver with the drunk who made the ambulance necessary in the first place."

Huber finds it distressing that technologically unsophisticated jurors are given the responsibility of determining whether a product—the Ford Pinto, for instance, or the Dalkon Shield—has been defectively designed and represents a danger to consumers. "Juries, and juries alone, are the final arbiters of defective design," he complains. According to Huber, juries have been asked "to redesign airplane engines and high-lift loaders, rewrite herbicide warnings, determine whether Bendectin causes birth defects, place a suitable price on sorrow and anguish, and administer an open-ended system of punitive fines."

Noting the reverence given the concept by the writers of the Constitution and the Bill of Rights, he asks, "Who could dare criticize the handiwork of such a venerable and respected institution? Vox populi, vox dei. Or, perhaps, vox Mother Goose."

Huber dares. Who has this awesome responsibility of determining whether products work as their manufacturers say? Not "the pharmacologists at the FDA (Federal Drug Administration)," he writes, "or the toxicologists at the EPA (Environmental Protection Agency), or mechanical engineers at the FAA (Federal Aviation Administration), but . . . the juror, pulled off the voter lists at random, solemnly sworn to his duty, and instantly educated in a contest of courtroom experts—solemnly sworn too, of course, and paid by the hour for their particular form of swearing. The member of the public judged incompetent to make wise choices in the marketplace for himself was now being called upon to make wise choices in the jury box for others. It was a theory of the idiot/genius, incapable of dealing with the objects that lay within his own experience, but infinitely capable of errorless flash judgment when it came to the experience of others."

Who better, G.K. Chesterton asked in his essay *Twelve Men:* "Our civilization has decided, and very justly decided, that determining the guilt or innocence of men is a thing too important to be trusted to trained men. . . . When it wants a library catalogued, or the solar system discovered, or any trifle of that kind, it uses up its specialists. But when it wishes anything done which is really serious, it collects twelve of the ordinary men standing around."

Huber and others who so ardently attack the civil justice system disagree with Chesterton. It is the "expert" who should have the final word on such matters as public safety, they say. But the Ford Pinto met federal safety standards devised by experts, and experts have approved other products for manufacture and sale with harmful and sometimes lethal consequences. Chemicals have been approved for use by experts in the Environmental Protection Agency and drugs by experts in the Food and Drug Administration, only to be proven deadly. It took juries of common people, provided with both sides of an issue, and asked to sort fact from fiction and determine right from wrong, to remove those products from the market or cause them to be redesigned.

Legal scholar Rita James Simon assembled a number of analyses of the jury in *The Jury System in America* and observed in her summary that many of the writers believed that jurors "grow up to their office . . . ordinary citizens sitting in their own homes might not have the wisdom and the interest to consider the issues, to weigh the arguments, and to debate the pros and cons of a particular case; but that these same citizens when collected by their government to serve as representatives of the public to the judiciary assume quite a different posture. Once they are selected for jury duty, their collective vision seems to expand and deepen, their reasoning takes on additional dimensions, and their ability and willingness to empathize and understand the feelings and life situations of others increases."

A University of Chicago jury project in the 1950s came to a similar conclusion, Simon wrote. The researchers found that a jury "takes its responsibility seriously; it checks many of its prejudices at the door of the jury room; it recognizes its special role as temporary members of the judiciary bound by rules of law and procedures not present in their business transactions or informal conversations.

"The fact is that ordinary citizens are willing to accept those trappings and work within them. The fears voiced by critics that jurors are led by bias, incompetence, and irrelevant facts to make capricious decisions are not substantiated."

That was more than 30 years ago. More recently, the Institute for Civil Justice of the Rand Corporation in Santa Monica performed a new study of jury verdicts. "Our research," Rand's 1985 report concluded, "shows that juries are usually sensible, and decisions have been remarkably stable over 20 years."

In any society there will be disputes that people cannot resolve between themselves. The bottom line, is where do you want to vest society's ultimate authority? We could, as other countries have done, vest total authority to resolve those disputes with judges or court magistrates. We could follow Peter Huber's suggestions and appoint "neutral panels" of experts in different fields. In taking either of those roads, however, we run a terrible risk.

Judges and magistrates must be either appointed or elected. Either way, the potential exists of political bias or favoritism towards one special interest or another. And we know from history that a judiciary freed from the balancing constraints of a jury system can easily become an oppressor rather than an objective arbiter.

In Germany, during the Third Reich, the courts did not close down. Judges did little to resist the implementation of unjust laws. Instead, they acted in concert with the political winds of the day and abdicated their sacred trust.

Relying on a special class of "experts" to resolve disputes and determine accountability offers little hope of better results, as Chesterton said. There is always the little matter of right and wrong in civil cases; and an engineer or a medical doctor or, yes, even a lawyer or a judge, is no better able to determine that than an ordinary citizen placed in a jury box.

The right to a jury trial is cradled in the heart of our Bill of Rights for a very practical reason—it is the only guarantee that justice will remain, literally, in the hands of the people.

"A jury," Murray Kempton wrote, "however humanly fallible, is our final repository for the experience of a personal sense of what is just and right, and every lobbyist who labors to restrict its liberty of judgment is at work on the denial of justice."

12

LAWYERS LESS THAN NOBLE

Four centuries after Shakespeare had a character say, "First thing we do, let's kill all the lawyers," a comedian came up with this variation on the theme: "Car insurance companies should give a discount," the performer said during the fall of 1988, "to anyone who runs over a trial lawyer."

Hilarious. I'm sure the spouse and children of every trial lawyer in the country laughed themselves silly.

Now, I'm not suggesting that comedians are acting in concert with the insurance industry when they include lawyer jokes in their routines. But they know they'll get a laugh with a lawyer joke. Lawyers have been in season for comedians for some years now, in good part because a sort of "climate" has been established by insurers, the medical community, and big business generally, which has made lawyer-bashing a major element in their anti-civil justice system campaign.

You know the themes. Lawyers chasing after ambulances and giving their business cards to the injured persons lying in the street. Lawyers filing frivolous, off-the-wall cases. Lawyers persuading a client to reject an acceptable settlement offer to gamble on a higher award from a jury. Lawyers stringing along a small-fee client and concentrating on a big-fee case. Lawyers cutting deals with other lawyers. Lawyers hiding evidence. Lawyers faking evidence. Lawyers walking away from a case with more money than their clients.

And on and on. Unfortunately, there are lawyers who do those reprehensible things; and I suppose it's a sound strategy for the interests trying to deform the civil justice system to try making the public believe most lawyers are that way, so they can be persuaded something must be done to keep the wicked ones in check. And while the intensity of the lawyer-bashing may have increased in the defense lobby's frantic effort to slam the door of the courthouse shut to the victims they create, targeting lawyers for abuse is not new, as the Shakespeare quote indicates.

It's painful for an attorney to acknowledge, but it is a fact that historically, although many of the most respected leaders of the various nations of the world—including our own—have been lawyers, lawyers in general have not always experienced a high level of respect by the societies they serve.

It's true there are attorneys who take advantage of their clients and of the situations in which the clients find themselves. There *are* attorneys who are simply opportunists and who exploit the difficulties of clients for their own personal gain. I firmly believe, however, that attorneys who are involved in those kinds of activities constitute a small minority; and that the great majority of lawyers are ethical, hardworking, and honest.

Lawyers are subject to the same criminal statutes as all other citizens, and in addition are subject to the standards of ethics developed by such professional associations as the American Bar Association and the 50 state bar organizations. Disciplinary committees created by each state bar hear complaints about attorneys from citizens, and when discipline is imposed it is reported in the monthly bar publications and in the legal press. The kind of questionable activities I've alluded to are no secret. I'm going to discuss some of them here to illustrate the difference between the right way of practicing law and the wrong way, so that consumers and victims can be aware of unethical practices and can report them when they're found.

A better understanding of the relationship between a client and an attorney, and their obligations to each other, will hopefully make it possible to eliminate or at least diminish abuses of the legal process so that the civil justice system can be made stronger. A stronger system will work better, be more fair, and assure that deserving people will continue to be served. The lawyer's role in the civil justice system can be strengthened, but it should be strengthened by constructive criticism, not impaired by a scornful, distrusting public.

Cries by so-called reformers of the system often include anecdotes of abuse by lawyers in an attempt to convince the public that the majority of lawyers are involved in questionable practices. If that part of the defense lobby's campaign succeeds, then major changes in the system might be tolerated. But it is not the system that should be the target of reformers; it is the abusers, and ethical lawyers will enthusiastically join in that effort.

Among the abusers are those lawyers who engage in the modern equivalent of ambulance chasing. In the old days, before electronic gadgetry became prevalent, quite literally some attorneys would chase an ambulance to a scene of an accident or intercept a patient at a hospital and offer representation to a victim. In modern times some attorneys have turned this into a near art form. An attorney, for example, might employ people whose primary function is to bring in business. The attorney might label these people "investigators" in an attempt to cloak them with some degree of respectability. The business-finders monitor police radio broadcasts so they can learn promptly when an accident occurs. They don't have to chase ambulances. Sometimes they reach the scene of an accident before the ambulance does in order to be the first to tell the victim, or victims, that an attorney should be obtained. And, of course, they know just the attorney. To illustrate the creative lengths some of these business-finders will go, a newspaper story a few years ago told of an incident in which officials discovered a priest ministering to survivors of an air crash wasn't a priest at all, but an "investigator" trying to sign up clients for his attorney-employer.

Such conduct is patently reprehensible. Immediately after an accident or onset of an illness, a person is usually in no condition to conduct the important business of contracting with a lawyer. He or she is usually confused, upset, sometimes under the influence of pain-killing drugs, and is not in a position to make an intelligent, informed decision when confronted by an attorney or a representative of an attorney.

Lawyers operating in this fashion have one objective: Get the subject's signature on the dotted line immediately and thereby tie up the representation of the client. Compounding this questionable tactic is the fact that many times these attorneys do not even intend to handle the case personally; rather, they use this process to accumulate clients they then refer to other attorneys, so they can collect what is known as a referral or forwarding fee.

Referring clients to other lawyers is not in itself unethical when the purpose is to help a client find an attorney who is better qualified to handle a particular case, or who can take another case at the moment. In practice, however, it is sometimes abused. The sad fact is there are attorneys who make a business of acquiring clients not for the purpose of representing them but rather for the purpose of referring them to another lawyer and collecting a referral fee.

People seeking an attorney should inquire into a lawyer's experience in actually representing, to final conclusion, other clients who have had similar problems. And, if the case involves a personal injury, they should determine whether the attorney has experience in handling, including trial, the same or similar kinds of personal injury cases. Many trial lawyers acquire expertise in handling claims involving specific injuries, such as, to the spine or to the head. This is not to say they couldn't handle a case involving an injury to another part of the body; it just means they have concentrated on cases involving those areas, usually because of acquiring a reputation for success.

I'm a California lawyer, so I'm familiar with the rules of conduct in my state, but I know that in many states, as in California, the referral of a client by one attorney to another requires the client's agreement. Most fee contracts, including contingency fee contracts, allow an attorney to associate other lawyers on the case without additional charge to the client. Whenever a case is referred by one attorney to another the client must be notified and have an opportunity to discuss the case with the attorney to whom the case is being referred. The client, upon learning of any such association or referral, always has the option of declining such representation. It is also required, at least in California, that any split of fees between lawyers in a referral or other situation must be approved in advance by the client.

A modern method of attracting clients, by television or radio advertising, is being used with increasing frequency. There are ethical attorneys who advertise their services in various ways, and after attracting clients in this fashion, deliver quality legal representation. Some advertising lawyers, however, are in fact nothing more than brokers. They have no intention of ever actually handling cases themselves, but advertise extensively and collect cases that they then screen and refer to other lawyers, for a fee.

A person seeking an attorney and responding to an advertisement should make the same inquiries discussed earlier relative to the lawyer's experience. The client should visit the attorney's facilities to determine whether it looks like a place where the business of the law is being done. A person can learn much from the general feeling received from visiting the attorney's office. I recommend that in all cases where it is possible the client visit the lawyer's office to make an assessment. A client should ask the attorney any questions that come to mind at this time. This, of course, includes the question of fees. An attorney who does not want to discuss fees or explain the reasons for a particular fee arrangement should be avoided.

One of the great successes in the delivery of legal services in America has been the contingency fee system. The system allows an injured person of poor or moderate means to obtain highly qualified representation by agreeing to give the attorney a percentage of any settlement or jury award received, if any. A great many people would be unable to afford the services of an attorney if this system were not available. Such fees are almost always negotiable, and should be discussed fully by the client and the attorney. California law requires a contingency fee arrangement be spelled out fully in a written contract between the attorney and the client, and neither side may change the arrangement without the approval of the other.

There have been instances of attorneys and their clients engaging in practices that amount to fraud on an insurance company. I do not believe this practice is widespread, but it does exist and should be recognized as an erosion of the civil justice system I've been discussing. Defrauding an insurance company can take a number of forms, including staging accidents, inventing injuries or exaggerating the severity of actual injuries, inflating medical bills, and claiming that there were more people injured in the accident than were actually involved.

Some lawyers have business arrangements with medical care providers or auto repair facilities and on occasion will insist that a client be treated for his or her injuries by a specific doctor, or that vehicle repairs be made by a specific garage. There is nothing inherently wrong in an attorney making a suggestion, particularly if the client has no funds immediately available for such treatment or repair, and the provider of service is willing to accept payment when the case is settled. But it is not acceptable, in my opinion, for an attorney to *require* as a condition of representation that the client do business with the businesses he or she recommends.

The medical profession, like the legal profession, has its bad apples, too, and bad apples are often attracted to each other. There have been reported instances where medical care providers have agreed to furnish false or fraudulent documentation with regard to the number of treatments received by the injured person or the extent or nature of the injury. In some cases this is done with the knowledge of the client and in some cases it is done without his or her knowledge. Any attorney found to be involved in such activity should be subject to swift and sure discipline by the bar and should be terminated immediately by any client involved in such a situation.

The reasons are simple. First, it is a crime to defraud an insurance company, and if the fraud is discovered, the client as well as the attorney (and the medical care provider) could be prosecuted. Second, if the attorney is acting unethically toward the defendant, why should the client think that lawyer would act ethically toward him or her?

Another deplorable activity practiced by a few attorneys is

claiming more persons were involved in the accident than actually were. This is called "packing" or "loading." When this occurs, it is usually in cooperation with a health care provider who will report "treatment" of these "injured" persons and present to the attorney medical documentation of the fictitious injuries and their treatment cost. This is another example of fraud and should not be condoned by either attorneys, their clients, the health care community, the insurance industry, or the general public.

Proper representation of an injured person by an attorney requires that the attorney interview the client to determine the facts of the accident from the client's perspective, and get an idea of the injury suffered. The lawyer should then investigate, through accident reports, witnesses, and other available sources, the facts of the accident in order to determine the extent to which the potential defendants may be liable. The attorney further has the obligation to acquire, from the medical or other health care provider, information about the nature and extent of the client's injury and the prognosis for the injured person's future.

The lawyer should also obtain financial information, such as wage loss and anything else that may have been an out-of-pocket expense of the client. Putting all of this information together, the attorney must work with the client in an attempt to determine the total value of the client's loss, including both the out-of-pocket expenses and other less tangible items such as the client's pain and suffering or loss of enjoyment of life.

It is not the attorney's job to build damages where there are none. An attorney must not attempt to suggest to a client that the value of the case can be increased by obtaining unnecessary or unreasonable medical or other health care services; nor should an attorney suggest that a client avoid returning to work when it would be otherwise appropriate for the client to get back on the job. If an attorney makes this type of suggestion, a client should immediately be suspicious of the lawyer's motives.

Management of the client's medical condition is the job of the health care provider charged with treating the patient's injuries, not the job of the attorney. This is not to say that a lawyer can't suggest a client may need medical attention in a particular area; but the attorney should not try to create the need for such medical attention or treatment, nor should he or she attempt to procure for the client medical treatment that is not necessary. An attorney may suggest the client see a particular medical or other health care specialist, but only the client's medical condition should dictate the kind of treatment obtained, and that decision must be made only by the client and the health care provider involved and not by the attorney.

Another area where there is potential for abuse is in case settlement. Sometimes an unscrupulous lawyer will attempt to talk a client into a settlement that is not in the best interests of the client but rather in the best interests of the attorney. A high degree of professionalism is to be expected of the attorney by the client in discussing the pros and cons of a particular settlement offer or particular settlement strategy. A client should carefully consider the attorney's advice in this regard because it is the attorney who has the expertise in this area. But the final decision is the client's, not the attorney's.

The potential for abuse here is that a bad attorney could attempt to settle the case for an amount less than appropriate in order to minimize the amount of work necessary to collect a fee. There are as many tactical decisions to be made as there are cases and it is difficult to draw distinct guidelines in this area. For instance, the settlement offer made by the defendant's lawyer may be considerably less than the victim sought, but the money would be received immediately. Going to trial could result in a larger jury award, but the defendant could appeal and stretch the case out for years before the victim receives a cent. The decision is not an easy one; but again, it is the client's to make, and it should be based on the client's best interests. If the attorney insists on a course of action, and the client does not agree, the client always has the option to change lawyers.

In California, where a client is represented by an attorney who is compensated on a contingency fee basis, changing attorneys will not cost the client additional money by way of fees. The second attorney will have to work out the potential fee split with the first attorney, if one is appropriate, and the client must be informed in writing and must agree in writing if there is to be a split. If there is a dispute between the attorneys or between the client and one or both of the attorneys, then the court becomes the final arbiter. Additionally, in California, the bar association for the local community is available to arbitrate fee disputes between clients and attorneys.

The relationship between an attorney and client must be one of trust and understanding, nurtured by free and open discussion regarding all aspects of the attorney's representation of the client. If an attorney is unwilling to engage in that kind of discussion, the client should consider looking elsewhere for representation. The client should expect an attorney to communicate on an understandable level and should feel comfortable that what has been discussed is fully understood. Attorneys become accustomed to using legal jargon, but when communicating with clients it is the attorney's obligation to do so in a way the client can fully understand. Clients who have difficulty with the English language should have the services of someone who can translate for them. Clients of limited education should ask plenty of questions so they are sure they understand what it is the attorney is attempting to tell them. Attorneys who will not communicate with their clients in an understandable way or who become abusive when asked questions should be looked upon with suspicion.

Perhaps the first question asked by persons needing the

assistance of an attorney is how to find one. It is natural for people needing a lawyer to want the best lawyer they can find, particularly when they know the lawyers on the other side are going to be experienced and competent. People needing a lawyer may be assisted in the search by talking to friends who may have had a similar problem, by consulting with lawyer reference services available in most communities, or by talking to attorneys who practice the type of law required. They also should discuss their needs with other people who may be familiar with the qualifications of various attorneys in the community.

If the client has doubts after initial discussions with an attorney, he or she should talk to other attorneys until one is found with whom a comfortable relationship is established. There is usually no charge by a personal injury plaintiff's lawyer for an initial consultation about potential representation, and if there is any uncertainty over whether there will be a charge, the client should simply ask in advance.

A person considering the services of an attorney should be wary of any who promise a certain amount of recovery at the first interview before all of the information necessary to make such an assessment has been obtained. A client should look with suspicion upon an attorney who makes outlandish statements or promises. The attorney should be expected to present himself or herself in a professional and straightforward manner and should be willing to discuss fully the potential representation and answer any questions the client may have.

A person looking for an attorney should keep in mind that the lawyer will be hired to work for him or her; and although the type of work being sought requires specialized training, expertise, and judgment not possessed by most lay people, it is the client who is the employer.

Above all, the client should remember that the case belongs to him or her, not to the attorney. Ultimate decisions regarding the case must be made by the client after full and careful consultation with the attorney as to all possible consequences of the options available.

It is the job of the attorney to protect the rights of the client and to employ the highest level of professional knowledge, expertise, and personal energy to get the client as full and fair a recovery as possible for whatever damage or injury has been done. If an attorney suggests fabrication of facts, medical bills, wage loss, or other aspects of the case, the client should not participate in such activity and should take steps to locate another lawyer immediately. It is not accepted practice, nor is it ethical, for an attorney to engage in such activity and such activity should not be condoned by the client.

All wrongdoing by lawyers is unethical; some wrongdoing is criminal. It's a fact of life, though, that if a police department or district attorney is faced with the alternative of prosecuting either murderers or people who claim they have personal injuries when they really don't, the limited prosecution resources will be expended on the more serious crime. That's as it should be. But there have been proposals on ways to accumulate funds for the prosecution of criminal fraud by attorneys and others in the personal injury field. Some of those proposals should be given serious consideration, and lawyers should lead the way in developing and supporting them.

Most of the proposals deal with creation of a self-funding mechanism—for instance, the earmarking of a small percentage of an auto insurance premium for a fraud prosecution fund. And, yes, perhaps earmarking for the same fund a small percentage of a lawyer's bar dues. Even if a mechanism can be developed and set in place and sufficient funds raised, it would all be meaningless unless an alarm is sounded where fraud is suspected, and the suspicion is investigated. It is the responsibility of every lawyer, plaintiff or defense, trial lawyer or not, to assist in exposing lawyers who violate the law or the canons of professional ethics every attorney pledges to observe.

Clients have a right to expect honesty from their lawyers. They also have a right to expect quality performance. When a client believes the quality of his attorney's performance has not been high, the civil justice system provides a remedy. Lawyers can be sued for malpractice by unhappy clients, just as doctors can. Attorneys who file medical malpractice suits complain constantly about the difficulty of finding doctors to testify against their colleagues. Lawyers should not allow a similar criticism to be directed at them. Attorneys unhappy about the public's negative perception of lawyers are going to have to help do something about that perception. And that includes helping weed out the bad apples who contribute to that negative perception.

I believe if it can be proven that a lawyer violated an ethical canon or guideline during his or her representation of a client, that fact should be admissible as evidence in a legal malpractice suit brought against the lawyer by the client. That kind of evidence— that a particular canon existed, and that a lawyer's conduct violated the canon—can come only from another lawyer serving as a witness in a malpractice trial.

There are always going to be people whose interests are served by attacking lawyers. One of the ways lawyers can make it more difficult for those critics to do that is to police themselves more vigorously. I realize it's easier to say that than to actually do it, but the stakes are very high, for each and every attorney and for each and every legal consumer, particularly those victims who turn to the civil justice system seeking fairness.

The system of civil justice we rely on for providing damages to victims of negligent acts in California is, as I have said before, a delicately balanced one. The system is designed to operate for the benefit of people who are injured by the negligence or disregard or deceit of another, but it must be managed in such a way that it is not taken advantage of by any person or entity involved in the process. If we can do this, then those who are made victims by the acts of others can retain the hope that the ones who made them victims will be held accountable.

If we can't, the losers will be those who are made victims. And any one of us, at any time, could become a victim.

13

MAKING A GOOD SYSTEM BETTER

The civil justice system so severely under attack by the defense lobby is, as we have seen, the product of centuries of evolution. And the histories of some of its components that are the primary targets of the attack—the jury trial, the contingency fee, and punitive damages—go back thousands of years. As a result of "legal evolution"—a constant sifting out of what doesn't work and refining of what does—the civil justice system we have today works pretty well. By and large, justice is done. Most of the time, wrongdoers are held accountable for the injuries they cause, and deserving victims generally are compensated for their injuries.

Lots of qualifying phrases in that last paragraph—"pretty well," "by and large," "most of the time," and "generally"— suggesting that the evolving civil justice system and the laws it applies still have a way to go before they are perfect. So, yes, reforms in the system are needed. But the reforms should make the system better, more efficient and *more* accessible to people, certainly not *less* accessible so the strong can be protected from the not-so-strong.

Legislatures, judges, lawyers, and many legal community organizations acknowledge that improvement is needed and address that need constantly. State legislatures across the country annually consider more than 5,000 bills dealing with the civil justice system. Local, state, and national trial lawyer organizations; bar associations; judges' organizations; and other members of the legal community across the country also constantly ponder proposals to make the civil justice system more easily accessible and more meaningful to people involved in a dispute.

The idea that the civil justice system should be made more easily accessible to victims probably gives the shivers to members of the defense lobby, who don't like being taken to court as often as they are now. I propose making them shiver even more by suggesting there are not enough competent trial lawyers in the country. True, in California alone there are some 115,000 licensed lawyers, but many of them do not practice law at all, many more are involved in government work, and still others are employed by corporations and do not handle litigation. Of the attorneys who practice trial work in tort cases, fewer than 1,000 of the 115,000 exclusively practice on behalf of plaintiffs in personal injury and related matters.

So, let me restate the suggestion: There are not enough competent *plaintiffs'* trial lawyers in the country.

The training of attorneys is often compared to the training of physicians, in that three or four years of education, followed by the passing of a difficult examination, is required after graduating from college before a license to practice can be obtained. In truth, however, the training is decidedly different. For many years, the medical profession has recognized specialties and required of doctors wishing to practice these specialties that they undergo additional training in their particular chosen field beyond the basic, general, medical education. After receiving training focusing on a particular field of medicine, a doctor must be tested and certified by a board of specialists before considering himself or herself a specialist in that field.

There is no similar program of specialized training within the legal profession, even though there are areas of law requiring specific expertise. Each lawyer is officially considered to be a generalist, and any restriction of an attorney's practice to a particular area—such as probate, tax, or corporation law, or plaintiffs' representation in personal injury cases—is voluntary.

I believe the legal profession should develop training programs similar to those of the medical profession for lawyers wishing to specialize, and to require certification before an attorney can claim to be a specialist. Certain areas of the practice of law require a great deal of education and study before a person becomes competent to specialize in them, certainly including trial work.

The best teachers of trial lawyers are time and experience, but law schools could give more emphasis to the teaching of primary trial skills in the courtroom. Law schools properly concentrate on teaching students the theory of law, but too little time is spent on teaching the other nuts and bolts of legal practice. Most attorneys leave law school without even the most rudimentary knowledge of how to prepare and file and prosecute a lawsuit. Much more attention needs to be paid to the actual development of a case for trial, including the techniques of discovery, so that vital information can be recognized and obtained and important witnesses identified.

The interrogation of hostile and friendly witnesses; the making of timely motions; the knowledge of how to develop a trial record for possible appeal, how to appeal, and how to oppose appeals and motions for dismissal and new trials are among the skills potential trial lawyers should be required to demonstrate before being allowed to represent a client in court.

165

It should never be forgotten that participation in a trial is often of monumental importance to a plaintiff. Its outcome—in the cases of Mary Anne Rodriguez and Richard Grimshaw, for instance—might well determine how the plaintiff is going to be able to live for the rest of his or her life. The plaintiff in a personal injury suit—and, of course, in any lawsuit—is entitled to representation of a quality at least equal to that employed by the defense. Allowing a plaintiff's lawyer who only occasionally goes to trial to go up against an experienced defense lawyer whose skills have been sharpened by frequent courtroom combat is not fair to the plaintiff. Remember, the plaintiff is already a victim.

But instead of improving, we are moving backwards. For example, voir dire (literally, to speak the truth) is the process of questioning potential jurors to assure that the 12 citizens empaneled will listen with open minds and deliberate in all fairness. It is a vital element to a good jury trial. But today far too few lawyers understand, much less successfully practice, good voir dire techniques. And too few judges who share the task and responsibility for selecting a fair and impartial jury give that part of their jobs serious enough attention.

As a result, the process of voir dire itself has come under attack. In the name of efficiency, some critics of voir dire want to exclude the questioning of jurors by the attorneys completely. It might save time, but at a tremendous cost. It goes without saying that if the jury system is the foundation of justice, the selection of a fair and impartial jury is essential to the healthy maintenance of that foundation.

How could Mary Anne Rodriguez have gotten a fair hearing from a jury that included those who were prejudiced against Hispanics or believed women are the property of men? How could Richard Grimshaw have gotten a fair hearing from a jury with a Ford executive on it? Voir dire allows the trial lawyers for both sides to weed out prospective jurors with damaging prejudices or other personal histories that might get in the way of their objectivity.

Our system of justice is an adversarial one. Two sides, both convinced they are right, marshall their evidence, prepare their cases, and present them to a jury for a decision. Who better than the opposing attorneys to fully understand the potential areas of bias that must be looked into before a fair and impartial jury can be selected? We need to improve voir dire, not eliminate it. Both judges and lawyers should be required to complete special training in voir dire before they are allowed to participate in a jury trial.

The question of education and standards also comes up in a relatively recently developed marketing tactic employed by some lawyers: advertising. Lawyers are constitutionally free to advertise if they wish, and lawyers who advertise are subject to the same truth-in-advertising laws as any other commercial enterprise. The problem is, the legal profession hasn't yet come to grips with problems created by advertising.

For instance, any attorney can claim in a television or radio or newspaper advertisement to be a plaintiff's personal injury trial lawyer, even with zero experience in a courtroom. Any attorney can claim to be a tax lawyer, or a divorce lawyer, or a criminal defense lawyer, or whatever, and there is no requirement for specific experience and competence in those fields. As I said, all lawyers are considered to be generalists, meaning they are supposed to be able to practice any kind of law. Setting standards, and requiring that advertised claims of specialization be limited to fields in which an attorney has met those standards, would be a service to and a protection for the legal consumer. It should be done.

Requiring specific education for lawyers wishing to engage in civil trial work, either for the plaintiff or the defense, would be a major step in the right direction. But improvement of the profession shouldn't stop there. In California, the Legislature, the State Bar, and the California Trial Lawyers Association have been exploring the concept of a mandatory continuing legal education program, generally based on the principle that each lawyer be required to obtain a prescribed number of hours of continuing education each year or some longer specified period of time.

There are already many opportunities for continuing legal education in most states, but, like the decision to specialize, participation is voluntary. For example, state trial associations regularly offer seminars and advocacy colleges, as do many private education facilities. Some lawyers—usually, the good lawyers—avail themselves of such opportunities. But too many lawyers lose touch with the developments in the law and advanced trial techniques necessary to aggressively represent their clients. If more law students can be attracted to trial work, if they can receive specialized training, if a special certificate must be obtained before a lawyer can represent a plaintiff or a defendant in a trial, if quality continuing education programs can continue to be available and more lawyers can be persuaded or required to take advantage of them, then the quantity and quality of trial lawyers will increase. And hopefully, many of those will represent plaintiffs.

Which leads to another problem, probably the problem most familiar to people both inside and outside the legal community: court congestion. It is distressingly true that years may sometimes elapse between the time a civil lawsuit is filed and the time the case finally goes to trial. The reason is simple: Population increases have added to the number of criminals, victims, divorces, and business disputes, all requiring court time. Existing court facilities are inadequate to meet the increased need, but politicians sensitive to voters' reluctance to pay more taxes have refused to raise the tax money necessary to enable the criminal and civil justice systems to meet that need.

The judicial system increasingly has become the orphan branch of government. The executive and legislative branches allocate the money, and they take care of their priorities first.

Few people fully understand what the judicial system does and how it operates, and since by definition it is outside the realm of politics, when there are budget crunches the third branch of government rarely is able to hold its own in the battle for dollars.

Coupled with the gradual penny pinching and unwillingness of legislators and governors to add the judges and courtrooms necessary to keep up with the population increase, the constitutional promise of swift justice gives criminal cases priority over civil ones. The result: Civil cases are delayed.

One simple answer is to increase the number of courtrooms and judges so that each case, civil as well as criminal, could be heard in a timely manner. It is necessary, it is important, and unfortunately, as I said earlier, it is also politically and economically impractical. One immoral answer is to curtail the number of legitimate lawsuits. But, as I have said, curtailing the number of legitimate lawsuits filed by restricting contingency fees or punitive damages won't diminish the number of victims being created every day, just their opportunity to take their grievances to court and have someone held accountable.

The answer (easier to say than to achieve) is to increase the efficiency of the courts. Several proposals are being explored, some of them controversial. They include giving greater stress to pretrial settlement, using what disparaging critics call "rent-a-judges" to arbitrate issues, and various "fast-track" proposals to hasten resolutions.

A few years ago California enacted a Trial Court Delay Reduction Program aimed at reducing congestion, but lawyers complained that judges weren't implementing it uniformly and within a year its effectiveness was questioned. The pilot program is scheduled to terminate in 1990 unless the Legislature extends its life. Whatever happens with the specific program, the experience with it will undoubtedly prove helpful in developing future delay reduction efforts.

Constructive efforts to improve the civil justice system are being made, and despite the arrogant assertions to the contrary by the defense lobby, the motive for those efforts is to make the system more accessible and more valuable to society generally, not simply more convenient for lawyers. Improvements are being made, but more are needed. The civil justice system is where people should go when they seek fairness. It is the place where they should find it.

14

IMPROVING THE LAW ITSELF

"The law," Mr. Bumble said, "is a ass—a idiot."

The law may well have been "a ass" when Charles Dickens wrote *Oliver Twist* in 1838 and gave that now-famous line to Mr. Bumble, but, as I hope I've demonstrated convincingly, it has come a long way in the century and a half since. Like the constantly developing and improving civil justice system I discussed in Chapter 13, however, the law itself can be better than it is.

The cases of Richard Grimshaw and Lily Gray graphically illustrate one current deficiency in civil law. Richard Grimshaw was mutilated when the Ford Pinto in which he was a passenger was struck from behind and exploded into flames. A jury decided that the Ford Motor Company had been, to be kind, negligent in designing the vehicle and should be assessed punitive damages to punish it and deter it from continuing to market the car. Lily Gray died in the same flames, ignited by the same design defect that caused such grievous injury to Richard Grimshaw. But if Lily Gray had been the only occupant, Ford could not have been assessed $3.5 million in damages to punish it and to deter it from continuing to market the Pinto, because the law in most states holds that punitive damages are not available to the survivors in a wrongful death.

Let me give you another example. A drunk driver runs over a pedestrian and causes serious injury. Punitive damages could be imposed if it could be proven that the driver knew he or she was drunk and insisted on driving anyway. But suppose the drunk driver, having hit and injured the pedestrian, decides to finish the job and backs up to run over the pedestrian again and the pedestrian dies. No punitive damages!

You can alter that scenario any way you want, but the illogic of the law in this case is apparent. If punitive damages are valuable to society because they punish the wrongdoer and deter the wrong-doer and others from similar wrongdoing in the future, what does it matter if the injured victim survives or not? This is an anomaly in the law, where it exists, and has been addressed frequently by trial lawyers with little success. It will continue to be addressed, and eventually, like the right of a woman to be an independent legal entity and the right of citizens to sue their government, will find its place in the law.

Illustrations of other loopholes in the law that favor civil wrongdoers could be cited from every state. But the point is that, despite all the improvements in the law over the years, there are still inadequacies that remain to be addressed. For instance, let's go back to the drunk driver for a moment. Doesn't it make sense that the provider of the alcohol that got the driver drunk has a responsibility, too? If the provider or bartender gives someone enough alcohol to become drunk, continues to provide alcohol until the drinker is obviously drunk—the test—and then lets the drunk climb into a car and drive away, someone injured—or the family of someone killed—by that driver should be able to sue the supplier of the drinks. What better way to make those suppliers aware of the potential danger they're exposing the community to than by requiring them to share responsibility if injuries, or deaths, result?

The issue has been presented to legislatures and to courts, with minimal success. Eventually, victims and their families will be able to hold suppliers of alcoholic beverages responsible, because it is right and it is fair, and that's what the law strives to be.

We're talking a perfect world, here, I realize, but we're also talking striving, reaching, working for perfection, for what is right and fair, and even if we don't make it, the one-step-at-a-time we travel while trying, is of value.

Another example: The law in every state requires that children be educated, or at least be given the opportunity to be educated. Fine. But sick children and hungry children don't have the same opportunity to learn that healthy, nourished, children do. Many states address half of that problem by providing hot breakfasts and lunches for children from families that can't afford to provide those meals themselves. Doesn't it make sense to address the other half as well? While federal and state legislatures are wrestling with the incredibly expensive issue of universal health care, shouldn't they meanwhile provide that health care will be available for any child who needs it?

That's the kind of a decision a legislature should make. But, as courts have held time and time again, if a legislature is paralyzed by competing interests from acting logically and constructively on an issue, and a question dealing with that issue is presented to a court in such a way that it can make a ruling that accomplishes what a legislature could not, the court will do just that. It might take a trial lawyer representing a child to bring the issue of health care for children to a court, but one way or another we are eventuality, as a society, going to take better care of the health of our children because it is right and fair.

Everybody has his or her own list of changes that would make Things The Way They Should Be. Those are some of mine.

There's another battle that engages trial lawyers that I haven't discussed yet, and that's the fight to recover rights once won that have been taken away. As I've said, the defense lobby has scored some frightening victories in its war against our civil justice system. While changes in tort law over the years have generally expanded the legal rights of victims and cemented the concept that individuals or businesses that cause injuries should be held accountable for the consequences of those injuries, there has been an occasional step backward, away from accountability, away from responsibility.

California, for instance, has long had in its statutes the Fair Claims Practices Act, requiring good faith efforts to settle insurance claims fairly. In 1979, the California Supreme Court decided in *Royal Globe Insurance Company v. Superior Court* that insurance companies, under the Fair Claims Practices Act, not only had to deal fairly with their own policyholders, but also with people who had filed claims against one of their policyholders. For instance, if a vehicle were rear-ended at an intersection and its driver injured, the injured driver of the first car might file a lawsuit against the driver of the second car, and that case would be defended by the second driver's insurance company. Under the *Royal Globe* decision, the insurance company would be required to treat the injured person fairly and in good faith.

The Court's 1979 decision was logical as well as fair. Most often, in the real world, it is the injured "third party" claimant who is probably going to be the victim of any bad faith insurance practices that exist. The "second party," the policyholder, would probably have little contact with the case since it would be handled

174

by the insurance company's adjusters and lawyers.

Today, in California, insurance companies still must deal fairly and with good faith toward their own policyholders, but no longer have the same obligation toward an injured third party. In September 1988 the state Supreme Court, in *Moradi-Shalal v. Fireman's Fund Insurance Company*, reversed the nine-year-old decision, holding that injured persons who believe they are being treated unfairly should take their complaints to the California insurance commissioner, not the courts.

There is little reason for an aggrieved consumer to have confidence in the commissioner's office, however. In a stinging dissent to the majority opinion, Justice Stanley Mosk pointed out that in the history of the insurance commissioner's office in California, there has not been one case in which the commissioner disciplined an insurance company for unfair claims practices.

Court testimony in San Francisco late in 1989 lent astonishing support to Justice Mosk's dissent. Insurance department officials who testified under oath revealed that more than 35,000 complaints had been filed in previous years with the insurance commissioner, and that the commissioner's office dealt with them by simply stacking them up for six months and then throwing them away. The commissioner, Roxani Gillespie, was on record at the time as having said that the number of complaints received had not been significant.

The insurance industry nationwide welcomed the *Moradi-Shalal* decision, as might be expected. Another decision that was hailed by the defense lobby, the U.S. Supreme Court's decision in *Foley v. Interactive Data Corporation*, sharply limited wrongful termination suits. For years, the courts had held that a steady job was too precious a need to be subjected to the whims of capricious employers, but the court apparently felt that the strong needed more protection from the weak and withdrew from most employees fired for no apparent reason the right to force their employer to justify the action.

But while such steps backward from justice, from the point of view of victims, do happen from time to time, they occur too infrequently for members of the defense lobby. Those who would change the civil justice system to reduce accountability find that the legal process is too slow a way to achieve the "reforms" they desire.

What they do, then, is to continue unending pressure on Congress and on state legislatures to attack the entire range of law that protects the innocent victims of negligence.

Among the offices I've held in the California Trial Lawyers Association is legislative chairman, which requires me to keep track of proposals that affect lawyers in general, trial lawyers in particular, and the victims who are their clients. Hundreds of bills affecting the civil justice system are introduced each year, and I'm sure the same thing, proportionately, happens in the other 49 states. Some of the proposals sound very logical and attract immediate support from lawmakers, while other sound outrageous and elicit immediate opposition. The initial reaction often lasts only until the measure's real meaning is explained.

In 1987, for example, a bill was introduced in California expanding immunity from liability for counties and cities providing safety services at public beaches. That sounds reasonable, at first glance. Who would want to see a well-meaning lifeguard sued if a rescue attempt of a drowning person failed? Well, sometimes there's a reason. For instance, a community advertises its beaches in an effort to attract visitors by claiming, among other things, that the people who go to its beaches can feel secure because there are competent lifeguards on duty. But suppose the lifeguard, during a rescue attempt, sets out in a lifeboat that is leaky and not seaworthy because it hasn't been maintained properly. Suppose the ropes on the other safety equipment are old and frayed and break at the first strain. If a life that could have been saved is not saved because of negligence, shouldn't those responsible for the negligence be held accountable? Wouldn't the fear of being held accountable prompt a government to make sure its lifeboats and other safety equipment were in working condition?

Another 1987 bill that many citizens would have no quarrel with, at first glance, would make police departments and police officers immune from lawsuits filed by bystanders injured during a police pursuit. Hard to find fault with that one; who would want to see a police officer or department held liable for an injury or death accidentally caused while the officer was pursuing a fleeing murderer?

But the problem comes up when an officer is pursuing a suspect in a negligent manner, such as going through stop signs and stoplights without red lights or sirens, at an excessive rate of speed for the conditions, perhaps in violation of the department's own guidelines on what justifies a chase and how it should be conducted. If a city or a police department or a county or a sheriff's department knows it could be held financially accountable for the death of an innocent person, or for injuries to an innocent person where such negligence is involved, isn't it more likely to emphasize the requirement to observe pursuit guidelines to its officers?

As I said, there are hundreds of similar proposals introduced in California alone each year, and similar bills are introduced in every other state. The bulk of them do not provide additional protections for consumers and working people. The bulk of them do not increase the accountability of insurance companies and other businesses. The bulk of them do not increase access to the criminal justice system for victims. The bulk of them are opposed, vigorously, by trial lawyers and by other advocates for consumer and victims' rights.

The civil law has changed over the centuries and the process of change will continue. Consumers, working people, and trial lawyers want it to change in one way, members of the defense lobby want it to change in another. We'd better pay attention.

15

A CHOICE OF DIRECTION

"Victims," Jesse Jackson said in 1987, "must have unlimited access to courts, because they have unlimited access to pain."

I didn't include this quote earlier in the book because, frankly, Rev. Jackson said in those 14 eloquent words just about all I've been trying to say. I've tried to show just how our lives have been bettered because we have unlimited access to courts, the better to illustrate what our lives might be like if that access were restricted or eliminated. Only in courts—only there—can victims be *assured* of finding fairness. Only in courts can victims like Louisa Muskopf, Mary Anne Rodriguez, and Richard Grimshaw be *assured* of standing equal to the government of the State of California, to Bethlehem Steel and McDonnell-Douglas, to the Ford Motor Company.

The purpose of this book has been to alert citizens, those who have been victims and those who might someday be victims, that their access to the fairness that courts provide is in peril. Its intent is to warn citizens that if they become victims, their opportunity to have those who made them victims held accountable may be diminished.

Accountable, accountability, responsibility, that's what this entire conflict is all about. I'm not talking about the results of true accident, of mischance, of things that just happen. Sometimes terribly tragic things happen, and no one's to blame. I'm talking instead about terribly tragic things caused by the deliberate or negligent actions of a corporation or an individual who should have known better or done better, who could have prevented the tragedy.

The defense lobby likes to shake its collective head and bemoan the loss of the good old days when people accepted their fate quietly. But it is one thing to accept the unavoidable tragedies of life, and it is wholly another to suffer unnecessarily because someone did something wrong. The phrase the law uses is "reasonable foreseeability." We all—individuals, professionals, and corporations—have a duty to avoid doing anything that we should reasonably foresee would cause harm to others. If an injury-causing occurrence could reasonably have been foreseen, the corporation or individual in a position to foresee it and to act to prevent it should be held accountable if it takes place and injuries result.

Manufacturers, the medical and insurance industries, other elements in the business community, and sometimes, sadly, even governments, want to be able to do what they choose to do without being held responsible for the consequences when they put dollars ahead of safety or when they are negligent or when they refuse to honor contracts.

Their arguments in the anti-lawyer, anti-jury, anti-civil justice system campaign they've waged invite the conclusion that they're unhappy about being forced to include such factors as safety and fairness in their business decisions. They're certainly unhappy when they're called to account for failing to include safety and fairness in their business decisions and someone is injured as a result.

They apparently want the world to revert to a time when they could have their way, without question. Once, the king could do no wrong. The law changed that, and some people in government are not happy with the change. Caveat emptor—let the buyer beware—was once a settled rule of commerce. The law changed that, too, and it is an understatement to say that some in business are unhappy with the change. The law now says to manufacturers, hospitals, doctors, even to governments, "You have a duty to be careful." The law now says to insurance companies, "If you choose to show bad faith to a policyholder, a jury is empowered to make that decision very costly for you."

Unfortunately, manufacturers, hospitals, doctors, and others in the business community, as well as governments, sometimes fail to exercise due care, and victims are created. Unfortunately, sometimes insurance companies act in bad faith and refuse to pay benefits to which policyholders are entitled, and, once again, victims are created.

If the world and the people in it were the way common sense would have them be, if insurance companies paid just claims fully and in a timely manner, if safety for consumers and employees were given a higher priority, most of the disputes that currently occupy the civil justice system wouldn't exist and the system wouldn't be needed. But they do exist, and the system is needed. A person asserting that he or she is a victim of another's negligence or willful disregard for safety or bad faith must prove that assertion in a court of law if the accused disputes it. The person must assert, and prove, economic loss if he or she is seeking compensation. If the person is seeking compensation for non-economic loss—for pain and suffering, for instance—he or she must justify that claim. A considerable degree of technical expertise and creativity is required to make such claims in a legally appropriate manner, and then to prove them, and that is what a victim seeks from a trial lawyer.

It's a two-way street, of course. An accused corporation or individual who denies responsibility for a claimed injury is entitled to be represented in court, too. Defense lawyers representing the accused are paid handsomely to provide challenges to the assertions made by the accuser, to make sure that every contention is proved, every claim is justified, to possess considerable technical expertise and creativity. Under our civil justice system, a judge decides what a jury can legally consider; and the panel of 12 reasonable members of the community, whose presence is agreed to by lawyers for the two sides, decides if fault exists and if compensation is appropriate.

It's a pretty good system, and it's comforting to know it's there. But isn't it sad that it's needed? Isn't it sad that the buyer must constantly beware? Isn't it a shame that a consumer has to be on guard when he or she walks into a car dealer's showroom looking for a vehicle to purchase? Or wants to join a health club? Or take dance lessons? We all get notices in the mail telling lucky us that we've won something or other in a sweepstakes if only we'll visit the sender's resort, or buy some magazines, or send in $10 for this or that charity. Wonderful opportunities are offered. Beware! Good deals are everywhere. Beware!

Although the law has changed with respect to a seller's responsibility to a purchaser, thanks in great part to personal injury lawsuits, it still makes good sense for the buyer to continue to beware. Such publications as *Consumer Reports* and *Money* warn readers just about every month to read the fine print in insurance policies, credit card applications, bank loan contracts, and the like. Typical was the April 1989 issue of *Money*, which alerted investors how they could protect themselves from "the sharp bite of those submerged (broker's) fees."

I've always wondered why an auto mechanic—just to pick a vocation at random—who chortles when getting away with charging a customer for a repair not needed, perhaps not even made, doesn't realize that he or she is a consumer, too, just like the customer who is cheated. And if the refrigerator breaks down and a repair person comes calling and charges for repairs not needed, or perhaps not even made, doesn't the mechanic realize that cheating the garage customer contributes to the climate that motivates the refrigerator repair person to cheat?

Maybe the person whose car needed repairs has sold health insurance described as supplemental Medicare insurance to a senior citizen on a fixed income, knowing all the while that the health insurance isn't needed, merely duplicates the Medicare coverage, and won't benefit the elderly citizen one single dime. But after doing that, he or she will turn around and complain about the garage mechanic's ethics, blind to the fact that that behavior and the mechanic's are related.

Consumers are part of the problem, too. I recently read the results of a survey in which a substantial majority of the people questioned said they thought it was all right to cheat their insurance company. It's not all right, of course, and it contributes to the high cost of insurance, just as shoplifting increases the cost of retail merchandise. Somewhere along the line, you'd think, enlightened self-interest—common sense—would prevail and consumers and the people who deal with consumers would realize that the long-range benefits of dealing honestly with each other outweigh the immediate benefit of cheating.

Maybe someday. Right now, though, sad as it is, the reality is that in this world we all share, we must constantly be on guard. If we relax that guard, if we're too generous with our trust, if we're not very careful, we risk economic injury. Unfortunately, the most frequent victims of economic injury seem to be the most vulnerable: the aged on fixed incomes and the poor, those least able to afford an assault on their pocketbook.

There can be emotional pain associated with economic injury. The pain can be intense, as anyone who has been cheated out of all or a substantial part of their life savings can attest. It is not unreasonable to ask in a court of law that compensation be ordered for both the economic injury and the emotional pain. Pain is associated with physical injury, too, and emotional pain can also be a consequence. The more intense the physical pain, the longer it lasts, the greater is the emotional pain. Sometimes the emotional devastation vastly outweighs the physical pain, as in those cases where once healthy, active, people are sentenced to a life in a wheelchair. It is not unreasonable to ask in a court of law that compensation be ordered for the costs arising from the physical injury and for the damage from the related emotional pain.

And it is not unreasonable to ask, in those cases where the defendant has acted in callous disregard for public safety, as the Ford Motor Company did in the exploding Pinto gas tank case, that substantial punitive damages be imposed. Evidently, trial lawyers have been sufficiently successful in having punitive damages imposed that the defense lobby has assigned a high priority to limiting, or better, eliminating them in its anti-lawyer, anti-jury, anti-civil justice system campaign.

Naturally, there will not always be agreement about who did what to whom, and what the consequences were. The beauty of the civil justice system developed over the centuries for resolving such disputes is that it is truly neutral. A typical citizen and a neighbor quarrelling over who owns the fruit from a tree growing in one yard but spreading over the other face essentially the same rules when they take their dispute to court, as Richard Grimshaw did when he sued Ford.

Businesses know the law and the rules of court, of course. Large firms keep well-paid, experienced lawyers on the payroll to make sure that every right is obtained, every legal protection is availed, particularly from injured people making accusations of negligence, fraud, or bad faith. Insurance companies, for instance, move swiftly to seek the court system's help in protecting them from losing money through the payment of fraudulently claimed benefits.

That's the way it should be. Better a dispute go to court and a judge and a jury hear the two sides, deliberate, and reach a verdict than the insurance company simply show up on an accused policyholder's doorstep and cart away a television set or a couch or whatever as repayment for its claimed loss.

It is also better that a judge and jury listen to both sides when it is a policyholder who feels that an insurance company is not delivering what the policy promises. The civil justice system is a reasonable alternative for those personalities whose first inclination is to try obtaining the money they think is due them out of the hide of the salesperson who sold them the policy.

But what might seem reasonable to a disinterested observer doesn't always seem reasonable to insurance companies in particular and the business community in general. The idea that a policyholder can not only disagree with a company decision regarding coverage but actually haul the company into court and make it explain its decision seems to be regarded as some kind of heretical violation of a basic sacrament. Similarly, the idea that someone who has been physically or emotionally injured by a business entity's negligence or callous disregard for safety would not simply accept his or her bad fortune as just the hand dealt by life seems equally alien to some business mentalities.

Like so many other aspects of modern living, a double standard is employed. Business likes the civil justice system just fine when it is to its advantage to go to court. Business doesn't like the civil justice system at all if it doesn't want to be in court.

Thomas F. Lambert, in his 1988 monograph, *The Case for Punitive Damages,* said it well: "Most disquieting of all, the present drive to eviscerate punitive damages, financed by the industry and insurance sectors, is only one phalanx in the broad conspiracy to dismantle the general tort system. Those who yearn to write the obituary of the tort system, their surrogates, and legislative stalking horses, are in full cry these days. Trial lawyers have always served as the 'tribunes of the people.' They have acted . . . conspicuously, during the last generation, in exposing the asbestos scandal and that industry's avaricious inhumanity toward millions of workers, their family survivors, and members of the public. . . . (T)rial lawyers and the contemporary tort system emerged as the *only* effective and indispensable means for exposing and then defeating the disreputable asbestos conspiracy and its cover up, while at the same time providing compensation to victims and deterring future malfeasance. All the other institutional safeguards of our society had failed these hundreds of thousands of dead and dying victims of asbestos-related diseases. . . . If it had not been for the intervention of trial lawyers pressing for the sanctions of tort law and compensatory and punitive damages, the asbestos conspiracy would have been buried along with its victims."

The unfortunate fact is, as Lambert suggests, people do act improperly toward one another, sometimes improperly enough to cause injury. Society has decided how it wants its members to respond when injury is done. If the injury has occurred because of a criminal act, and a person has been accused of the crime, society wants the question of guilt or innocence, and punishment, if appropriate, determined by a court of law operating within the criminal justice system. If the injury was not caused by a criminal act, and a person or business or government has been accused of causing the injury, society wants the question of responsibility and of compensation, if appropriate, determined in a court of law operating within the civil justice system.

It seems to me the logical extension of the anti-lawyer, anti-jury, anti-civil justice system campaign being waged by the defense lobby, aimed at denying access to the civil justice system by victims of low or moderate means, would be to invite those victims to take matters into their own hands when they suffer injury, to seek not only compensation or restitution but revenge.

Isn't that where civilization was several thousand years ago? We must, as we have, take the higher road. Justice through law, truth through trial, progress through responsibility. Give up? We never have, we never will.

BIBLIOGRAPHY

A.M. Best Company. *Best's Aggregates and Averages.* New
    Jersey: A.M. Best Company, annual.

Bellotti, et. al. *An Analysis of the Cause of the Current Crisis of
    Unavailability and Unaffordability of Liability Insurance.*
    Washington D.C.: National Association of Attorneys
    General, May 1986.

Berman, Harold J., ed. *Talks on American Law.* New York:
    Vintage Books, 1961.

Blair, Kristin R. "Nader, Lawyers and Insurance." *Family, Law
    & Democracy Report* Feb. 1989.

Blom-Cooper, Louis, ed. *The Literature of the Law.* New York:
    The Macmillan Company, 1965.

---, ed. *The Language of the Law.* New York: The Macmillan
    Company, 1965.

Boorstin, Daniel J. *The Mysterious Science of the Law.* Boston:
    Beacon Press, 1941.

Brant, Irving. *The Bill of Rights.* New York: The Bobbs-Merrill
    Company, Inc., 1965.

Cahn, Edmond, ed. *The Great Rights.* New York: The Macmil
    lan Company, 1963.

Cooper, Dr. Mark J. "Trends in Liability Awards: Have Juries
    Run Wild?" Washington D.C.: Consumer Federation of
    America, May 1986.

Daniels, Stephen. "We're Not a Litigious Society." *Judges
    Journal* Spring 1985.

Ellis, Dorsey D. Jr. "Fairness and Efficiency in the Law of
    Punitive Damages." *University of Southern California
    Law Review* Nov. 1982.

Friedman, Lawrence M. *A History of American Law.* New
    York: Simon and Schuster, 1973.

Galanter, Marc. "Reading the Landscape of Disputes: What we Know and Don't Know (And Think We Know) About our Allegedly Contentious and Litigious Society." *U.C.L.A. Law Review* 31:4.

---. "The Day After the Litigation Explosion." *University of Wisconsin Institute for Legal Studies* Aug. 1986.

Hamilton, Alexander. *The Federalist (No. 83)*. New York: The Modern Library, 1937.

Huber, Peter W. *Liability, the Legal Revolution and Its Consequences*. New York: Basic Books, 1988.

Insurance Information Institute. *Insurance Facts: 1985-86 Property/Casualty Fact Book*. New York: I.I.I. 1987.

---. *Insurance Facts: 1986-87 Property/Casualty Fact Book*. New York: I.I.I. 1988.

---. *Insurance Facts: 1987-88 Property/Casualty Fact Book*. New York: I.I.I. 1989.

Insurance Service Organization, Inc. *Insurer Profitability—The Facts*. New York: Insurance Service Org., Feb. 1986.

Jefferson, Thomas. *Jefferson's Letters*. Arranged by Willson Whitman. Eau Claire, Wis.: E.M. Hale and Co., undated.

Kalven, Harry Jr., and Zeisel, Hans. *The American Jury*. Boston: Little Brown, 1966.

Kindregan, Charles P., and Swartz, Edward M. "The Assault on the Captive Consumer." *St. Mary's Law Journal* 1987.

Lambert, Thomas F. Jr. *The Case for Punitive Damages*. Washington, D.C.: Association of Trial Lawyers of America, 1988.

"The Litigation Explosion is a Myth." *Business Week* March 10, 1986.

Localio, Russell. "Variations on $962,258: The Misuse of Data on Medical Malpractice." *Law, Medicine and Health Care* June 1985.

Lowe, Robert F. *The Property/Casualty Insurance Industry.* Casualty Actuaries, Inc. 19 Feb. 1986.

Maitland, Frederic W. "Origins of Legal Institutions." *The Life of the Law.* Ed. John Honnold. London: The Free Press of Glencoe, 1964.

---. "The Development of Equity." *The Life of the Law.*

Moore, Lloyd E. *The Jury.* Cincinnati, Ohio: The W. H. Anderson Company, 1973.

Nader, Ralph. "The Trial Bar and the Public Interest." *Trial Lawyers Quarterly* 19 (1988).

National Center For State Courts. *A Preliminary Examination of Available Civil and Criminal Trend Data in State Trial Courts for 1978, 1981 and 1984.* Vermont: National Center for State Courts, April 1986.

National Underwriter. *National Underwriter* 1 Dec. 1984.

Nice, Richard W., ed. *Treasury of Law.* New York: Philosophical Library, Inc., 1964.

Peterson, M.A. *Compensation of Injuries.* Santa Monica: Rand Corporation, 1984.

Peterson, M.A., and Priest, G.L. *The Civil Jury, Trends in Trials and Verdicts, Cook County, Illinois, 1960-1979.* Santa Monica: Rand Corporation, 1982.

Salomon Brothers, Inc. *Property/Casualty Organizations: Five-Year Review and Outlook, 1985 Edition.* New York: Salomon Brothers, 1985.

Shanley, M.G., and Peterson, M.A. *Comparative Justice, Civil Jury Verdicts in San Francisco and Cook Counties 1959-1980.* Santa Monica: Rand Corporation, 1983.

Simon, Rita James, ed. *The Jury System in America.* Beverly Hills, CA: Saga Publications, 1975.

Simon, Rita James, ed. *The Jury: Its Role in American Society.* Lexington, MA: Lexington Books, 1980.

United States. Department of Justice. *Report of the Tort Policy Working Group on the Causes, Extent and Policy Implications of the Current Crisis in Insurance Availability and Affordability.* Washington: GPO, Feb. 1986.

---. Federal Courts, Administrative Office. *Annual Report for 1985.* Washington: GPO, 1985.

---. General Accounting Office. *Product Liability.* Washington: GPO, Jan. 1988.